MW01199344

Thomas K. Mugerditchian

The Diyarbekir Massacres
and Kurdish Atrocities

Gomidas Institute
London

© 2013 Gomidas Institute

ISBN 978-1-909382-07-7

Gomidas Institute
42 Blythe Rd.
London W14 0HA
United Kingdom
www.gomidas.org
info@gomidas.org

The Diyarbekir Massacres
and Kurdish Atrocities

TABLE OF CONTENTS

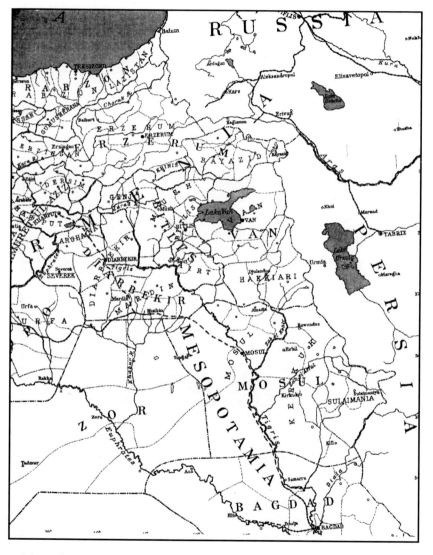

Map showing Diyarbekir province and beyond. Source: American
Geographical Society, cir. 1918. [Gomidas Institute reprint 2002]

With the author's respectful compliments.
Thomas K. Mugerditchian

THE DIARBEKIR MASSACRES.

and

KURDISH ATROCITIES.

०००००००००००००

By

THOMAS K. MUGERDITCHIAN.
(H.B.M.'s Ex Pro-Consul of Diarbekir.)

╈╈╈╈╈╈╈╈╈╈╈╈╈╈╈╈╈╈

CAIRO

1919.

Original cover page to *The Diyarbekir Massacres and Kurdish Atrocities*

Introduction

The Armenian Genocide as a Complex Process

Uğur Ümit Üngör

On the eve of the First World War, about two million Armenians lived in the Ottoman Empire. In the spring of 1915, the Ottoman government took a series of measures against its own Armenian citizens. At the end of the war, only a fraction of the pre-war Armenian community remained, as about three thousand Armenian settlements (villages, cities, districts) had been depopulated and their inhabitants massacred. Nowadays, outside Istanbul, almost no Armenians live in Turkey any longer. These rough facts sketch in a nutshell the complex history of the Armenian genocide.

The destruction of the Ottoman Armenians was a complex result of three important forces: military defeat and the loss of territory in the Balkans in 1912–13; the Young Turk coup d'état of 23 January 1913; and the outbreak of the First World War. The genocide developed out of the delusional fear of an organized Armenian insurrection, which reached boiling point when Allied forces landed on Gallipoli in the night of 23 to 24 April 1915. The next day, Interior Minister and CUP leader Mehmed Talaat Bey (1874-1921) ordered the arrest of the Armenian elites of the entire Ottoman Empire. In Istanbul, up to 300 Armenian intellectuals, clergymen, physicians, editors, businessmen, journalists, lawyers, teachers, and politicians were rounded up and deported to the interior. While the political prisoners were killed outright, the rest were sent further to die in the wastelands of Syria.[1]

---

[1] Some of the survivor accounts include Mikayel Shamtanchian, *The Fatal Night: An Eyewitness Account of the Extermination of Armenian Intellectuals in 1915* (Studio City, CA: H. and K. Majikian Publications, 2007); Aram Andonian, *Exile, Trauma and Death: On the Road to Chankiri with Komitas Vartabed* (London: Gomidas, 2010); "Monument to April 11" in Rita Soulahian-Kuymjian, *Teotig: Biography* (London: Gomidas Institute, 2012), Yervant Odian, *Accursed Years: My Exile and Return from Der Zor, 1914-1919* (London: Gomidas, 2009); Gregoris Balakian, *Golgotha: A Memoir of the Armenian Genocide, 1915-1918* (New York: Knopf, 2009).

As other provinces followed, the Armenian community became effectively decapitated of its political, intellectual, cultural, and religious elites. Decapitation of the Armenian community by mass executions of the economic, religious, political, and intellectual elite was the first pillar of the genocide. The great roundup in Istanbul of 24 April 1915 was to become a guideline for the arrests of the Armenian elites throughout the vast country. Almost all those detained were men of middle or advanced age with influence, wealth and status. They were imprisoned, often tortured, and finally murdered. For example, in the cities of Bitlis and Harput/Kharpert, all prominent Armenian men were arrested, transported to the suburbs, and shot dead. The bodies were thrown in trenches dug in advance.

Diyarbekir

One of the best-documented examples of the mass murder of Armenian elites is that of the south-eastern province Diyarbekir, home to approximately 106,000 Armenians. By May 1915, the fanatical CUP nationalist Dr. Mehmed Reshid (1873-1919) had imprisoned the entire Armenian elite of that city, where some had already died under torture in the citadel prison. Reshid administered the final blow to the elite in the last week of that month. On Sunday 30 May 1915 his militiamen handcuffed more than six hundred notables including the Armenian bishop, and led them through the Tigris Gate (*Dicle Kapı*). On the shores of the Tigris the men were loaded on 23 large rafts under the pretext that they would be relocated to Mosul. Militiamen sailed the notables downstream to a gorge where the rafts were moored. The victims were robbed of their money, taken away in groups of six, stripped of their clothes and valuables, and massacred by Kurdish tribesmen of the Raman tribe recruited by the governor. The perpetrators murdered them with axes, daggers and guns, and dumped the bodies in the river. The destruction of the Armenian intelligentsia was completed breathtakingly quickly: the entire top layer of the community was eliminated within weeks.[2]

Philibos Arpiarian was provincial director of the Ottoman Agricultural Bank who had worked in Kharpert, Trabzon, and was stationed in Diyarbekir when he was arrested in May 1915. When the deportation was announced, he sent the following letter to his family:

---

2 Uğur Ümit Üngör, *The Making of Modern Turkey: Nation and State in Eastern Anatolia, 1913-1950* (Oxford: Oxford University Press, 2011), chapter 3.

My Dears,

What is going to become of us is now clear. I will probably be sent toward Mosul, together with all my compatriots. Now it is left for you to be brave and endure every difficulty. What can we do? Fate brought us to this. Only continue to pray for us.

As for my journey, bring me one of the boy's sheets, a small rug, pillow, and two or three underclothes. My blue jacket and vest. In addition to this, my summer jacket, trousers, and whatever else is suitable to wear. I must not forget, also, a lot of cheese, choerag, and prepare a box of halvah.

Use your judgment and put all this together in the best way you can. Give these to Haji Garabed so he can bring to me. He is our servant. Bring a cognac bottle filled with oghi (raki) with you so you can pass it secretly to me. Do not be too late. All of you come so that I can see you for the last time.

Kisses to you, your father... Philibos Arpiarian[3]

The goods never reached Arpiarian but were stolen by the militia, and Arpiarian was placed on a raft and taken away with the other notables to be killed.

Arpiarian was one of 636 victims. Among those killed were Onnik Kazazian, a wholesaler from Istanbul who happened to be visiting Diyarbekir, and his friend Artin Kassabian, the former interpreter of the French vice-consulate. Other victims were the noted bankers Khatchadur Dikranian and the Tirpandjian brothers.[4] The same fate befell Mihran Basmajian, graduate of Euphrates College in Kharput, Dikran Chakijian, and Nalband Hagop, all of them Dashnak party members, as well as Hagop Hovsepian, the negotiator Stephan Matossian, former provincial interpreter and secondary school teacher Dikran Ilvanian, member of the municipal council and representative of Singer Missak Shirikjian, all of them members of the Ramgavar party.[5] The slaughter was breathtakingly fast and profound: the entire Armenian elite of Diyarbekir was effectively

3 Marion Tashjian-Quiroga, *The Tragic Years Remembered 1915-1920* (Troy, NY: The Printing Outlet, 2002), p. 67.
4 Report of M. Guys to the French embassy, Istanbul, 24 July 1915, in: Arthur Beylerian (ed.), *Les grandes puissances, l'empire ottoman et les arméniens dans les archives françaises (1914-1918): recueil de documents* (Paris: Université de Paris I, Pantheon-Sorbonne, 1983), p. 48, document no. 58.

wiped out within a week. To the dismay of Walter Holstein, the German vice-consul at Mosul, a week later the rafts arrived empty. Holstein later found out that the Christian convoys had been 'completely slaughtered' (*sämtlich abgeschlachtet*) and he had witnessed their corpses floating downstream: 'For several days, corpses and human limbs have been floating down the river here.'[6]

The Relevance of Mugerditchian's Book

The recent publication of the biography of Emînê Perîxanê (?-1933), noted chieftain of the Raman tribe, has shed new light on Kurdish involvement in the massacre. It was published by his son Hüseyin Demirer (1919-1983), who relied on his own memories and the social memory of his immediate family members. The Raman tribe reigned in the Kharzan valley and was famous for its female chieftain Perîxan. She had seven sons, who competed for succession: Mustafa, Said, Ali, Emîn, Abdullah, İbrahim, and Ömer.[7] In order to succeed their mother, the sons had to outclass each other in the ability to exert power and express leadership qualities.[8] Of all her sons, Ömer was known for his ferociousness and acumen. Before the war, his campaign of plunder, provocation of government forces, and bravado did not go unnoticed. In the summer of 1914, the government declared him *persona non grata* and ordered him arrested and incarcerated. Ömer escaped prosecution and retreated into the Kharzan region as an outlaw.[9] Conversely, his brother Emîn organized a paramilitary unit and in the winter of 1914 successfully fought with the Ottoman army on the Caucasus front.[10]

Dr. Reshid, according to his own memoirs, summoned Ömer for a secret mission in the spring of 1915. Ömer and Mustafa travelled to the

---

5 Thomas Mugerditchian, *Dikranagerdi Nahankin Charteru yev Kurderou Kazanoutiounneru* (Cairo: Djihanian, 1919), pp. 95-100.

6 *Politisches Archiv des Auswärtigen Amtes*, Botschaft Konstantinopel 169, Holstein to Wangenheim, 10 June 1915.

7 Hüseyin Demirer, *Ha Wer Delal: Emînê Perîxanê'nin Hayatı* (Istanbul: Avesta, 2008), pp. 63-4.

8 "Ji birakujiya nava eşîran nimûneyeke sosret: Emînê Perîxanê - Evdilê Birahîm," in: Salihê Kevirbirî, *Filîtê Qûto: Serpêhatî, Dîrok, Sosyolojî* (Istanbul: Pêrî, 2001); "Deng û Awaza Xerzan," in: *Özgür Politika*, 3 January 2000.

9 *Başbakanlık Osmanlı Arşivi*, DH.İD 80/5, Interior Ministry report, dated 8 August 1914.

10 Demirer, *Ha Wer Delal*, chapters 5 and 7.

governor's office in Diyarbekir, where terrified urbanites saw the outlaw and his intimidating entourage enter the city. Mugerditchian vividly described this atmosphere:

> Amero [Ömer] was of a short stature, darkish, with small-pox scars on his face. He wore a big turban on his head around which hung many coloured silk insignias to show that he was a Kurdish chief. He also wore a black short tunic (local made), long breeches, and red shoes... being armed with a Mauser rifle, two revolvers, a sword, a dagger, a *yataghan*, and carrying with him an enormous amount of bullets and cartridges.[11]

Dr. Reshid received them in his office and explained that the Armenians were stabbing the country in the back by helping the Russian army. The governor suggested that he would deliver convoys of Armenians to the brothers, who would escort the victims down the Tigris on rafts, ultimately to kill them all. If they agreed, they were entitled to half of the total booty on condition of absolute secrecy. Seduced by the prospect of abundant wealth, the brothers agreed and the plan was set in motion.[12]

After the massacre, Ömer and Mustafa were invited to the governor's house, where they celebrated their accomplishment and sold the expensive clothing they had taken from the victims in the bazaar.[13] Reshid also congratulated them for their "bravery, patriotism, and services to the state," and appealed to the Interior Ministry to have his militia rewarded and awarded medals for their outstanding performances. His wish was granted by the Directorate for General Security, and the militia members received financial benefits and were decorated with medals.[14] Three other convoys followed and were destroyed in a similar way. But Dr. Reshid had made the Pêrîxan brothers complicit in his crime and did not trust their loyalty. He ordered their execution: the brothers were set upon by his agents and killed in their sleep in the summer of 1915.[15] Their brother Emîn continued to work for the

---

11 Thomas Mugerditchian, *The Diyarbekir Massacres and Kurdish Atrocities* (London: Gomidas Institute, 2013) p. 37. For the original Armenian see *Dikranagerdee Nahankin Tcharteru yev Kurderou Kazanioutounneru* (Cairo: Djihanian, 1919), pp. 57-8.
12 Demirer, *Ha Wer Delal*, pp. 75-89.
13 *Politisches Archiv des Auswärtigen Amtes*, R14087, director of the Deutschen Hülfsbundes für christliches Liebeswerk im Orient (Frankfurt am Main) Friedrich Schuchardt to the Auswärtiges Amt, 21 August 1915, enclosure no. 6.

government but would not fare well either: he was eliminated by the Kemalist government in 1933.

Until the publication of Demirer's memoir, the details of the Diyarbekir massacre were murky. It is now clear that the Kurdish perpetrator "Amero" in Thomas Mugerditchian's memoir and "Ömerê Pêrixanê" in Kurdish oral history are one and the same person. In other words, Mugerditchian's account of the Diyarbekir massacres corresponds with and cross-corroborates all other sources on the Armenian genocide in that province. The book contributes to increasing consensus in Armenian genocide studies that the Diyarbekir killings are among the most unequivocally documented massacres of the genocidal process.

---

14 *Başbakanlık Osmanlı Arşivi*, DH.EUM.MEM 67/31, 27 July 1915. Deputies Aziz Feyzi and Zülfü Bey, and militia Major Şevki were decorated with honorary medals for their "great achievements". *Başbakanlık Osmanlı Arşivi*, DH.KMS 43/10, 11 January 1917. According to a British intelligence report, "Deputy Feyzi was received by the Kaiser and decorated with the Iron Cross". *National Archives* (UK), FO 371/4172/24597, no. 63490, folio 304.
15 Demirer, *Ha Wer Delal*, p. 87.

Note from the Editor

Ara Sarafian

The Diyarbekir Massacres by Thomas K. Mugerditchian can be found in the archives of the United States Department of State.[16] It is a typed manuscript composed of four sections: (1) the author's personal experiences in Diyarbekir up to November 1914;[17] (2) the genocide of Armenians and Assyrians in 1915 based on the testimonies of Levon Kassabian, Thomas Donjian, as well as Julia and Selma Ispir; (3) lists of people who were murdered in Diyarbekir, Mardin and elsewhere during this period; and (4) the author's own assessment of the origins of Kurdish tribes in the Diyarbekir region.

The Diyarbekir Massacres makes for fascinating reading, not least because its author was a former British Vice-Consul in Diyarbekir, a savvy observer, and a good writer. He gave a great deal of information about the events leading up to 1915, as well as details about the manner in which atrocities were organised, including the names of hundreds of perpetrators and victims. The culprits included the political leaders of Diyarbekir province, lower ranking officials and civilian murderers. This

---

16 *The Diyarbekir Massacres* was originally printed in Armenian. While it is not clear who translated the work into English, Mugerditchian was clearly involved in the process: the typed manuscript sent to the State Department included his handwritten corrections; the photographs accompanying his text included his handwritten captions; and the title page included his handwritten compliments and signature (see p. viii). The State Department Index Bureau recorded receipt of this manuscript on 24 October 1919. For the original English translation see United States National Archives, General Records of the Department of State, RG 59, 867.4016/417. For the original Armenian publication see Tovmas K. Mgrdichian, *Dikranagerdi Nahanki Charteru yev Kiurderou Kazanoutiunneru (Aganadesi Badmoutiun)* [The Massacres of Dikranagerd (Diyarbekir) Province and the Bestialities of Kurds (Eyewitness Account)], Cairo: Krikor Jihanian Press, 1919.

17 As a British consular employee, Mugerditchian fled the Ottoman Empire in November 1914, when the Ottoman Turks entered World War I against the Allied Powers. He spent the war years in Cairo, Egypt.

work is one of the earliest narratives of the Armenian Genocide for any part of the Ottoman Empire, and the detailed observations the author managed to collate for his report is remarkable.[18] As a result, *The Diyarbekir Massacres* can be subject to critical analysis and corroboration with other primary sources.[19]

Despite the serious nature of the report, Mugerditchian does not write in a cold and dispassionate style. Rather, he reflects the pain, suffering and frustration of many Armenians, and pleads for his nation. Like many Armenian intellectuals in 1919, he clearly believes that the future security of Armenians lay in an independent Armenian state.[20] This was an understandable sentiment given the horrors visited upon Armenians in

---

18 Mugerditchian's focus was on the destruction of Armenians, especially those residing in the city of Diyarbekir, so that he did not include a great deal of information on the destruction of Assyrians (including Chaldeans). However, many of the victims he mentions by name were Assyrian.

19 Hüseyin Demirer, *Ha Wer Delal, Eminê Perîxanê'nin Hayatı*, (Istanbul, Avesta Yayınları, 2008); Üngör, Uğur (2005), *CUP Rule in Diyarbekir Province, 1913-1923* (University of Amsterdam, Master's Thesis, 2005); Ara Sarafian, "The Disasters of Mardin During the Persecutions of the Christians, especially the Armenians, 1915," in *Haigazian Armenological Review* 18, Beyrouth, 1998; Statements by Floyd O. Smith (Diyarbekir) and Alpheus N. I. Andrus (Mardin) in James Barton, *Turkish Atrocities: Statements of American Missionaries on the Destruction of Christian Communities in Ottoman Turkey, 1915-1917* (London: Gomidas Institute, 1998), pp. 87-104; Henry Riggs, *Days of Tragedy in Armenia: Personal Experiences in Harpoot, 1915-1917* (London: Gomidas Institute, 1997), pp. 51-61; Arthur Beylerian, *Les grandes puissances, l'Empire ottoman et les Arméniens dans les archives françaises (1914-1918)*, (Paris: Publications de la Sorbonne, 1983); Rafael Nogales, *Four Years beneath the Crescent* (London: Sterndale Classics, 2003 [reprint]). For a more nuanced account based on Armenian sources see Raymond Kevorkian, *The Armenian Genocide: A Complete History*, London: I. B. Tauris, 2011, pp. 355-380. I am also grateful to have seen a manuscript on the Diyarbekir massacres by Hilmar Kaiser.

20 While some Armenians were ideologically predisposed to support such an Armenian state, many others, such as Mugerditchian, did so on practical grounds: By 1918 the mass murder of Armenians had taken its devastating toll, the people who had carried out the destruction had not been brought to account, and there was no serious possibility of survivors returning to their former homes.

Diyarbekir, as well as other parts of the Ottoman Empire, between 1915-18. The possibility of an independent Armenia had already been voiced by the Allied Powers during the Great War, and writers such as Mugerditchian reminded their audiences of these promises. Indeed, Mugerditchian may well have sent the English translation of his work to the United States Department of State for such purposes.[21]

Despite the political undertones of his work, *The Diyarbekir Massacres* remains a fascinating account that is worthy of serious examination. In 2013, based on information Mugerditchian provided, the present writer was able to locate the exact location where a group of 635 Armenians from Diyarbekir were murdered in June, 1915.

Editorial Note

The Diyarbekir Massacres was translated into English rather quickly. This is apparent in the poor language and spelling, as well as its overall presentation. Although we have corrected some of the English, we had to be circumspect and the original language has remained largely intact.

While reviewing the manuscript, we found minor discrepancies between the Armenian original and its English translation. It was not always clear whether the differences were errors of translation or corrections by the author. Consequently, any information we have added into the English translation from the original Armenian has been placed in square brackets or appears in footnotes followed by the initials of the current editor "—A.S."

Regarding the spelling of Armenian, Turkish and Kurdish proper nouns, we have standardised some of these according to conventional English usage (eg. changing the sounds "tch" to "ch", "dj" to "j"). We have also used an Armenian transliteration table where needed (see p. 77), and in some cases, we have left nouns as in Mugerditchian's original translation.

Finally, Mugerditchian sent his manuscript to the State Department with a separate batch of photographs which depicted people and places mentioned in his text, as well as images related to the treatment of Armenians in 1915. Some of these photographs were clearly staged while others could not be verified. Such photographs have not been reproduced

---

21 In 1919 there were expectations that the United States, under the presidency of Woodrow Wilson, would assume a mandate over such an Armenian state at the forthcoming Paris peace talks.

in the present publication due to their lack of authenticity or provenance. However, we have used six photographs, which we believe to be authentic, and placed them in Mugrditchian's text at our discretion. I wish to thank Anika Patel, Pietro Shakarian and Ercan Yurtsever for their help when preparing this work.[22]

---

22 For a critical discussion of the staged photographs, see Abraham D. Krikorian and Eugene L. Taylor, "The Saga Surrounding a Forged Photograph from the Era of the Armenian Genocide Demonizing and Vilifying a 'Cruel Turkish Official': A part of 'the rest of the story.' at *http://groong.usc.edu/orig/ak-20100222.pdf*

The Diyarbekir Massacres
and Kurdish Atrocities

[PART I]

My Dear Wife,[*]

In compliance with the request which you sent me after you went from Baku to London, I am herewith sending you an account of the Diyarbekir atrocities, massacres, etc., which I collected from the following two eye-witnesses, both of whom are natives of Diyarbekir.

(1). Levon Kassabian, youngest son of Haji Haroutiune Kassabian, Pro-Consul and Dragoman of the French Consulate at Diyarbekir.

(2). Thomas Donjian, son of Hovhannes Donjian, Silk Merchant at Diyarbekir.

The latter remained at Diyarbekir up to the 18th of July 1915, when he was deported. Miraculously he escaped and made his way to Aleppo, where he is still living. The former by extraordinary courage hid himself in all possible hiding places and managed to remain in Diyarbekir up to the 7th of December 1917, on which date, disguised as a Kurd, he left Diyarbekir and walked to Mardin and from there to Ras-el-Ain, and from this last place to Aleppo, where he reported to the U.S. consul, Mr. Jackson, who was a pronounced friend of the Armenians. Mr. Jackson afforded him every possible facility and protection and finally sent him off safely to the American "Syrian Protestant College" of Beyrout.[†] After many hardships, adventures and privations he finally reached Cairo on the 16th of March 1919. Both these men not only admit and confirm all the terrible stories which your published narrative "From Turkish Toils" contains, but also give such other frightful accounts of persecution and massacres that are enough to drive one mad.

---

[*] Mugerditchian framed his work as a response to a book his wife wrote describing her escape to the Caucasus with their children in 1914-15. See Esther Mugerditchian, *From Turkish Toils: the Narrative of an Armenian Family's Escape,* (New York: George H. Dorian Co.), [n.d.] —A.S.

[†] The Armenian text also states that Levon Kassabian was sent off as a student with an American passport. —A.S.

It is to be wondered at how the Armenians who remained in Diyarbekir heard, as I am told, of my flight to Egypt and of my present sojourn in this city (Cairo), as well as of your escape with our six children to Tiflis. Poor men! They had all along been hoping that you would do something through the assistance of General Antranig for their deliverance. The Turkish authorities and the Turkish and Kurdish population of Diyarbekir gnashed their teeth when the news of our family's escape reached them while the Armenians were mightily surprised and considered our escape nothing less than a miracle.

Thomas K. Mugerditchian

I am sorry that this time I have no happy news to communicate to you, but only heart-rending stories, the nature of which is not, however, wholly unknown to you, as you have also been yourself an eye-witness and have been with our six children through that blood-stained trail and through that very same valley of the shadow of death. Our successful escape is indeed a miracle, and we must forever thank and praise God for having thus helped us through.

My heart and soul are full of agony for this affliction incomparable with any other plague which has smitten our nation. History will look with horror upon the crimes committed, and humanity will unanimously condemn the work of the infidel Germans, and the dog-hearted and brutal Turks, who united to knead the whole world with fire and blood.

I believe it will be quite appropriate to prefix my own experience up to the 1st of November 1914, (the date on which I went away from Diyarbekir), to the narration of these two eye-witnesses.

Yours affectionately,

[initialed] K.

P.S. Further and more complete information has also been recently received and included in the attached account from the following sisters, Julia and Selma, daughters of Prof. Eblahad Ispir (a Protestant Greek) of the American High School at Mardin. These two sisters with their children left Mardin in May 1918 and went to Aleppo, where the cost of living was comparatively cheaper. In June 1919 they arrived in Cairo.

[initialed] T.K.M.*

---

* The Armenian text is dated Cairo, July, 1919 —A.S.

Historical.

Past Claims of Armenians Concerning the Safety of their Persons and Property

During the last three quarters of the 19th century and the opening of the 20th century Armenians experienced bitter persecutions and more than once became victims to the most outrageous carnage. After the gallant resistance which the handful sons of Zeitoun offered in 1862 against 50,000 Turks who pressed hard upon them, surrounding them on the mountains where those brave souls still fought and kept their dignity and valour like eagles, the European Powers were somehow stirred up and interfered on behalf of the Armenian defenders, extracting a few "stingy" privileges on behalf of the heroes.

The world also heard of the Sassoun Movement in 1893-1894, when Serop Pasha, Kachën (gallant) Antranig, and Damadian with a handful of valiant boys built their nests on the rocky peaks around the villages of Dalvorig, Shenik, Semal, Gelie-Gouzan, Andok, and Vir-Vir Kar, from where they helped, encouraged and protected the Armenian inhabitants of these villages against all attacks from the ever-savage, and ever-ferocious Kurdish brigands. When Sultan Abdul Hamid heard of this, he was naturally alarmed, because the facts were monstrously misrepresented to him. He then immediately sent whole armies with guns and ammunition to go to the assistance of the native Kurdish tribes and suppress the Armenian movement. In a short time his men covered the whole of Sassoun like locusts. Every village and habitable place was at once invaded, pillaged and burnt to the ground. The losses inflicted on the Armenians, the public exposition of Serop Pasha's head, and the tremendous number of other victims, again attracted the niggard attention of the Great Powers of Europe. Representatives were at once sent to Moush and Sourp Garabed. As a result, a substance-less dummy called "Reforms," was granted to the six Armenian vilayets.

The first outcome of this "Reforms" scheme was the general massacre of 1895 in the six vilayets and of 1896 in Constantinople, right under the nose of the Ambassadors of the Great Powers, who had a chance of becoming eye-witnesses of the lamentable result of the dummy Reforms. The loss of 300,000 Armenians with their large properties was duly registered in the diplomatic books of the Great Powers, and a few lines added to the pages of history, and that was all about this matter.

Turkish constitutional liberties were proclaimed in July 23rd 1908. Muslims and "Rayas", Turks and Armenians, Albanians and Kurds, Arabs and Jews and Gypsies rejoiced and danced and kissed each other. The reactionary movement of March 31st 1909 followed. The Young Turks' army marched to and was welcomed in Constantinople. The Red Sultan was dethroned and Turkish liberty was once more set in her right place. Suddenly a red curtain spread over Adana. New massacres of Armenians, new devastations, new tears and blood. The honourable representatives of the Great Powers in Turkey once again opened their diplomatic books and registered, under the previous numbers that had for years been entered on the page of "Armenian Massacres," the new figure of 30,000 more victims. As for the commandants of the European warships that happened to be in Turkish waters, they were good enough to remember to take a few photographs of the victims.

Is it necessary to say more about the devastations that were wrought by Turkey? For the past [blank] and half centuries, and especially for the last two and half centuries, she had lost bridle and reins and run a wild race shedding blood and scattering destruction and sighs and groans everywhere. As a consequence of these oppressions and trials which the European Powers tolerated, the Armenian tribe of Rushdounik, unwilling to forsake their father's homes and move to a distant and safe place, changed their religion and were thereafter known as the Kurdish tribe of Reshkota. Other Armenian tribes followed their example, so that the tribe of Pakradounik was changed into the Kurdish Bakëra, the Mamigonian into Mamëga, the Alyan into Alëka, the Mogats into Motga, while the Armenian and Assyrian population of Jebel-Tor (Tor-Abdin), under the leadership of the Jacobite Patriarch Ismayel, were forced to change their religion and establish the Kurdish tribe of

Mahallemi,[*] on which occasion the Patriarch assumed the title and duties of Sheikh Ismayel and continued to be the Chief of his Muslim tribesmen.[†]

Fortunately the great majority of the Armenians remained firm on the rock of their faith, unmovable in the midst of the most stormy whirlwind of persecution and distress which the Turks blew and drove over them. Having come out of many fiery a furnace, they have maintained their national existence and unity up to the present day. Notwithstanding all that they suffered at the hands of the Turks, the Armenians for ages continued to serve them loyally. They rebuilt many times what the Turks had reduced to ruins; they promoted trade and industries and rendered valuable services to the Turkish government even along political lines. The two Amiras Kazaz Haroutiun and Douzian, the Patriarchs Nerses Varjabedian and Haroutiun, Krikor Aghaton, Servichen, Balian, Hagop Pasha, Artin Pasha Dadian, Odabashian, Odian, Portoukalian, Baroutji Bashi Dr. Nafilian Pasha and a large number of others did all that was possible for the maintenance and continuation of the decaying Turkish Empire.

Never did Armenians show any tendency towards severing their union with Turkey. What they wished and planned for, and rightfully asked from the Turkish government, *was a guarantee for their own personal safety, and for the security of their property, nothing else.* Instead of treating this natural and innocent request fairly, the Turkish government considered it a revolutionary attempt to quench and took such steps as cannot be forgiven. The result of the oppressive policy assumed by Turkish authorities was the immediate springing up of several Armenian National Committees, to which the Turks gave the name of and considered as revolutionary. These Committees were organised with the sole purpose of becoming the advocates for the rights, needs and desires

* The Armenian text explains that the Mahallemi are actually a Beylik, as opposed to the other groups, which are tribes —A.S.
† In the Armenian text the author states that he has given more information about these tribes at the end of this book —A.S.

of Armenians and for pleading their cause with the authorities. They further tried to ameliorate the condition of the oppressed Armenian peasants, who were never free from the raids and persecutions of the Kurds, and to help the government in spotting out the unworthy and unreliable Government officials who allowed or encouraged such unlawful acts.

But the Armenian nation generally speaking was weak and without resources, while these Committees, which undertook to plead the cause of Armenians, were new and inexperienced. Besides, they lacked the means, the tact and the power to present their holy cause sufficiently strongly before the High Courts of the European Powers, who alone could solve their question. And so the Armenian problem known in diplomatic language as "Reform in the Six Asiatic Vilayets of Turkey" remained forever on the green tables of the various cabinets, altogether untouched and always constituting a modern Gordian Knot.

The last universal war that shook the very foundations of the whole world was precipitated on July 28th 1914. The whole earth was changed into a dismal Hades and its inhabitants into ferocious animals. The nations surpassed each other in discovering different means for killing and destroying the other. Seas and oceans, rivers and lakes were coloured red. Yet nowhere, nothing could surpass the monstrosity of the Turks in their exterminative understanding against Armenians. No record can be found in the history of the world which will begin to compare with the ill-treatment, suffering and tortures that the Armenian nation passed through.

The Germans – the Huns of Europe – and the Turks – the Mongols of Asia – formed an alliance which splendidly suited each other. They then competed, the former in Belgium and the latter in Armenia, as to who should commit the greatest atrocities and the most horrible crimes. The Germans, personified in "Haji" Wilhelm, and the brutal Turks, personified in the Committee of Union of Progress, will remain under the curses and the anathema of the nations whose innocent blood they shed "till moon shall wax and wane no more."

Mobilisation, Recruiting and Despatching of Troops

The mobilisation of the Turkish Army was ordered on Monday, the 3rd
of August 1914 and the subsequent Imperial Decree for recruiting and
despatching men arrived in Diyarbekir on the following day, 4th August
1914. As in every other part of Turkey, so in Diyarbekir and in every
village of the vilayet, on the arrival of this order, owing to previous orders
and arrangements, both secret and open, which had come months earlier,
the mobilisation of the Turkish Army was immediately put into effect at
a rapid rate, as if pushed on by a spring. Thus, with the immediate
mobilisation and movement of troops, Diyarbekir presented the picture
of a boiling kettle. On the evening of the same day, that is on Tuesday
the 4th of August, another Imperial decree arrived ordering the whole of
Turkey to be put under martial law. It is therefore on this day that the
open persecutions began.

Requisitioning

Immediately following the organisation of the Military Recruiting
Commission, the Requisitioning Committee was also formed. The
steersman of this committee was the director of the Committee of Union
and Progress club of Diyarbekir, Attar Hakki Effendi, assisted by the chief
representative of this same Club, [*Miurakas*] Jirjis Agha Zade Kior Yussuf
Bey. Both these men were natives of Diyarbekir. The Requisitioning
Committee immediately established branches in every village of the vilayet
by means of telegraphic instructions.

The purpose of this Committee was to confiscate in the name of
"military necessities," all the property of merchants and shop-keepers,
without exception, whether large or small. They thus confiscated all the
available raw and wrought cotton and wool; all the raw iron and copper,
as well as tools, dishes and plates made of them; sugar, tea, coffee,
matches, timber, all kinds of fats, oil, petroleum, wheat, barley, millet,
rice, cotton, horses, camels, mares, mules, donkeys, cows, buffaloes,
goats, oxen, sheep, carpets, rugs, blankets, etc. All this wholesale
requisitioning was carried out, as I mentioned above, under the name of
"military necessities." Briefly, within a few months, all the Armenian

stores, depots and shops were robbed of their contents: the large supplies of wheat and barley which were kept in every house and well – for wells are widely used as storing places – were taken away, the stables were left without any cattle whatsoever, and all these were stored in government and CUP stores in the various centres of the vilayet. The officials entrusted with the supervision of this work were selected by the Committee of Union and Progress. In return for all this confiscated property a piece of paper bearing the signature of some unknown or insignificant clerk of the Committee of Union Progress was given promising payment at the end of the war.

In the meantime all Armenian artisans were employed without any payment in military and civilian establishments and factories for the production and preparation of such things that the local Government required.

Vali Jelal Bey Prevents a Demonstration

On the 9th of August, I called on His Excellency the Governor Jelal Bey to whom I mentioned in a friendly way that, in accordance with information I had from different reliable sources, the Committee of Union and Progress was planning to organise and hold a demonstration on the following day, which would parade through the main streets of the town and the market, and finally go and protest in front of the British Consulate against the commandeering of the Turkish dreadnoughts "Sultan Osman the Invincible" and "Reshadieh," which were being built for Turkey at Portsmouth. I called His Excellency's attention to the fact that in case of such a demonstration actually being held by savage men of the Kurdish type, the results would be deplorable, and that the chief person who would then be held responsible for such disorders would not be any of the Committee of Union Progress instigators, nor any of the mob, but very naturally His Excellency himself, whom we all considered to be a good and friendly Governor and would not like to see in such an unpleasant position. His Excellency, after having verified the truth of my report, issued the necessary orders and the demonstration was not allowed to be held.

The Renaissance Company

The attention of the Committee of Union and Progress had long ago been drawn to the fact that the whole of the commercial, industrial and manufacturing enterprises of the country were in the hands of Armenians. On account of this, the Committee of Union and Progress took the initiative of forming a company, membership to which was limited to Muslims only, under the name of *Intibah Shirketi* (The Renaissance Company). Their purpose was to usurp at any cost the commercial, industrial and manufacturing supremacy which had been held throughout the vilayet by Armenians, as well as to lay hands on the import and export trade of the vilayet, which was a chief source of wealth, also carried on by Armenians. Being, however, inexperienced, and naturally incapable for, and ignorant of such enterprises, and having been born to earn by easy work a living which would supply their daily comforts, pleasure and luxuries without any other higher ideals, they could not compete with the well-known commercial genius of Armenians. Thus the Renaissance Company failed to accomplish its original purpose but was kept alive with plans and schemes which had failed in the first attempt but kept always ready "on the desk" for a more suitable opportunity for implementation.

The Market is Burned

The enforcement of Martial Law in Diyarbekir, as in every other part Turkey, presented an excellent opportunity to the agents of the Renaissance Company to usurp according to their instinctive nature – that is force and oppression – what they had proven themselves unable to master by honest work, competition and perseverance. Furthermore, in order to inflict a death blow to Armenian Commercial prosperity and dry up all resources for any future progress of Armenians, the Director of the Renaissance Company Parliamentary Deputy Pirinchi Zade Feizy Bey, acting on instructions from the Committee of Union and Progress, worked out an elaborate plan for the burning of the market. This plan was put into execution on the night of 19 August 1914, under the direction and with the personal aid and assistance of the Police

Commissioner Guevranli Zade Memdouh Bey. Within five hours 1,080 shops, 13 bakeries, two inns, 14 lumber depots etc. were reduced to ashes. To understand the enormity of the losses incurred by this fire, let one bear in mind what the government and the municipality authorities of Diyarbekir wired on 31 August 1914 to the Higher Authorities in Constantinople, i.e. that the losses arising out of the market fire amounted to 350,000 Turkish pounds. The investigations, however, of the French and British Consulates based on the statements of experienced merchants, well versed in the affairs of the market merchants, estimated the losses at a full half a million Turkish pounds. It must also be borne in mind that the owners of the sixty-one Muslim shops were duly informed and had in time transferred to a safe place all the contents of their shops.[*]

Deputy Feizy Bey Speaks

On Thursday the 27th of August 1914 I paid a visit to Deputy Feizy Bey at his own home, where I also met his uncle Mufti Ibrahim Effendi. On this occasion we continued at length the discussion which we had started a few days before, when he and his friend, the ex-Mayor of Diyarbekir Deputy Kiamil Effendi,[†] came to have tea with us at the British Consulate. Although Feizy Bey always wanted to appear as a friend of the British Consul and of Great Britain in general, he was not discreet nor prudent enough to conceal his deeper and real feelings. In the course of our conversation I asked him what he thought about the European War, whether Turkey would participate in it, and in case she did participate, with whom would she side. Without any hesitation or reservation Feizy Bey said: "The whole world is going to participate in this war. The Germans have made such tremendously big preparations, and have discovered so many new "destructive implements," such as bombs, guns, submarines, aeroplanes, zeppelins, money, soldiers, etc., that there is not the least doubt that Germany will win in the end. They first of all crush France, then Russia, and then, before your friends the British have had time enough to prepare themselves for defense, they will turn upon them.

* The Armenian text mentions 60 Muslim shops —A.S.
† The Armenian text does not say Kiamil, but Kemal. —A.S.

The interests of Turkey dictate that we should side with Germany. The Germans have promised, in case of our co-operating with them, to restore to us all our lost territories, that is Egypt, Tripoli, Tunis, Algiers, the Caucasus, Thrace, Macedonia, Crete, Cyprus, the Islands of the Aegean, and in addition to all these, they will give us India. Then we shall establish a Great Ottoman Empire comprising lands occupied by 300 million Muslims. Then... Your greedy British friends, on the other hand, did not even give us our own two dreadnoughts, commandeering them for their own use!"

I called his attention to the reasonable question, that Turkey ought not to view only possible German successes and victories, but also German failures and defeats. If Germany came out defeated at the end, what would Turkey do? By siding with Germany she would naturally become the enemy of her traditional friend, Great Britain, who had saved her three times from sure death, and in case of Germany losing the game, Turkey would also lose everything. If, on the other hand, Turkey remained, at least neutral, she would lose nothing, as her integrity had been guaranteed, and would at the same time materially enrich her own people.

At this point, Feizy Bey, ignoring my questions, abruptly changed the subject of conversation and turned to the Armenian question. He said that the whole Armenian nation and the Armenian Committees had openly declared themselves in sympathy with the cause of Great Britain and her Allies; that this was a great mistake and folly for the Armenians; that they should not forget that they were primarily Turkish subjects; and that they would do well if, through the Armenians of the Caucasus, they could create some kind or other disturbances in that part of Russia, so that the Caucasus could be detached from Russia and joined to Turkey. I replied that as long as Kars and Ardahan were under the Russian Government, Armenians became rich and prosperous. As an example of Turkish misrule I mentioned to him the six Turkish vilayets, the most important part of the inhabitants of which are ever sighing under the heel of the savage and wild Kurd, where there exists neither personal safety, nor safety of any kind for property. The Turkish Government would therefore do better, if it granted comparatively greater freedom and extension of privileges to the Armenians, and by doing this Turkey would serve both her own interests, and at the time present a model of a well-governed place to the Armenians of the Caucasus. As if he did not hear my last words, he went on with his own remarks, saying that if the Armenians insisted on their foolish game, they would ultimately pay a high price for it. Russia, France, and Great Britain cannot help them, and cannot, and will not be able to save them, while Turkey is in a position, free and capable to do whatever she wants in the matter, without either Austria or Germany ever saying a word of protest about it. I told him that he was using exceptionally open language, to which he replied that last spring he had gone with a commission composed of members of the Turkish Parliament to Berlin, and that his words were the impressions and the natural conclusion of what he then saw, heard and learned. To close the conversation in a friendly manner I told Feizy Bey: "You are a clever man, and you know that if you want to have every day milk and eggs for your breakfast, you must feed the cows and the hens. Is it not so? The Armenians have all along rendered valuable services to Turkey."

On another occasion Feizy Bey and his friend Deputy Kiamil Bey came to a tea party at the British Consulate. During our conversation I pointed out to them that the Requisitioning Commission would pretty soon swallow up all the wealth and all the property of the Armenians; that many acts of injustice had been committed, and that they as representatives of the Muslim and Christians of Diyarbekir alike, could advise the heads of the Requisitioning Commission, Yussef and Hakki Effendis, who were their friends and strongly under their influence, to put an end to all such excesses, because, I said, if they meant to seize the property and wealth of Armenians in this manner, they would soon discover that they had drained all the commercial, industrial and agricultural sources of the country's wealth, which undoubtedly constituted the chief source of income for any country which might find herself engaged in war. Thus they would destroy and kill not only the Armenian prosperity but Turkey herself. "Well," he said, "let the Armenians think so. They are few, and if these few are destroyed, the whole nation will be wiped out of existence. But we are many, and if even half of us perish, the other half will still remain in its place. Moreover, we will finally win more than what we have lost during the last 200 years."

To change the tone of the conversation I told him: "It seems that you came here only to displease me today. But remember that Germany will grip you, and you will become her slaves. They are a poor and hungry nation and they will swallow you up. It will be much profitable and wiser to trust your parents' friends, than to risk the untried feelings of new and poor friends."

Interview with the Head of the Requisitioning Commission

On the 10th of September 1914 I called on the most influential member of the Requisitioning Commission, its President Jirjis [*Agha*] Zade Kior Yussf Bey, to whom I remarked that since the existing proportion between the population of Diyarbekir was two Muslims to one Christian, the weight of the requisitioning ought to be divided at the same rate, whereas the examination of his books would readily show that five out of six persons whose property had been requisitioned were Armenians and one, and that nominally, a Muslim. He replied, "The Armenians are rich, the market and the bazaars, the trade and professions of all sorts, and the agriculture of the Diyarbekir town and vilayet are in the hands of the Armenians. They have plenty of money. Let them give!"

I mentioned to him, as examples, the names of several of the Kurdish chiefs, beys, pashas, etc. both in the town and in the vilayet of Diyarbekir who had proportionately larger fortunes and bigger amounts of ready cash, and that justice and right ought to be applied equally in every case so that some proportion might be established in this case of requisitioning too. I further said that by destroying the Armenians they were killing the hen that laid the golden eggs for them.

The Secret of Major Mustak Bey's Suicide

On Tuesday morning, September 15th 1914, the report was widely circulated that the Staff-Major of the 23rd Regiment, stationed at Diyarbekir, Major Mustak Bey, had blown his brains out and had been found dead in his bedroom. Soon the truth of the report was ascertained. Three letters, dated September 14th were also found on his desk, and when read, they disclosed the secret of his suicide. One of the letters was addressed to his wife at Constantinople, the second to his brother, who was a captain serving at Van, and the third to the G.O.C. Troops, Diyarbekir. The contents of these three letters were almost identical. He first of all protested against the excesses committed by the Requisitioning Commission against the poor population, blaming those responsible as acting wholly unjustly and arbitrarily, especially against the Armenians. Then, in strong language, he condemned the secret instructions which had come from the Headquarters of the Army Corps at Erzingian, under date of July 10th, requesting the Military Authorities at Diyarbekir to heavily oppress and persecute the Armenians,[*] and concluded by saying: "Unable to accept such mean and unjust orders, although sanctioned by the Turkish Government, and approved by the Muslim element, and being a conscientious Muslim, I cannot any longer tolerate such evil and iniquity; I am ashamed to bear any longer the name of Turk, and I put an end to my life."

Vali Hamid Bey

The new governor of Diyarbekir Hamid Bey, a native of Rodosto [Tekfurdag], arrived at Diyarbekir on the 1st of October 1914. He had previously been the Mustessarif of Kirk-Killisa and the Dardanelles [Chanak Kale], for some time Civil Inspector of a Adrianople [Edirne], and last of all Assistant to Mr. R. Graves, then Chief Representative in Constantinople of the General International Inspection Commission for Turkey. There was indeed a great need for such a strong and active hand as that of Hamid Bey because, since the last Governor had left on August 16th, the Kadi had taken charge of duties temporarily and being an extreme fanatic had allowed everything to slip from his hand into those of the foolish administrators of the Committee of Union and Progress.

---

[*] The Armenian text states *shnchasbar unel* or smother Armenians. —A.S.

Hamid Bey immediately on his arrival arrested the Police Commissioner Memdouh Bey, on whom the whole responsibility for the fire of the market lay, and exiled him to Adana. He also had a large number of Kurdish chiefs arrested and imprisoned among whom were Sarhan, Ali Butie, Hajo, Moustafa, son of Tamogawri, and others, because these were the most influential and powerful Kurdish brigands in the neighbourhood of Tor Abdin. These had never recognised the existing authorities and kept the whole vilayet in a condition of constant terror and unrest. They did not even pay the least attention to the mobilisation order of the Recruiting Offices.

This sensible and active Vali came several times to the British Consulate and exchanged opinions on different matters with the Consul. When once the subject of Turkish political relations was touched he did not hesitate to declare that Turkey was not as foolish as to forsake her traditional friend and liberator, Great Britain, and throw herself into the arms of Germany, which meant nothing else but a sure suicide for the Turkish nation. He admitted, however, that the three leaders of the Committee of Union and Progress and the present [sic] dictators of Turkey were openly pro-German: sold, blind tools in the hands of the Germans.

My Flight

During October 1914, when you were still in Harpoot, I wrote to you several times saying that there was every reason to believe that Turkey would soon join the Central Powers, and that in view of this, the British Consul planned to go abroad, and that naturally I would do my best to go with him. As a result of the abrogation of the Capitulations I had lost the privilege of British protection which I had enjoyed throughout the vilayets of Diyarbekir and Harput during my 19 years' employment in the Consular service, first as a dragoman, and later as a Pro-Consul. In those letters I had repeatedly asked you to take our six children from the American Schools of Harput and come at once to Diyarbekir so that we might all get away together with the British Consul. Unfortunately for us the Turks suddenly plunged themselves into the war and the British

Consul was obliged to leave Turkey at once. Being convinced that my remaining in Turkey would, on account of my long and faithful services to Great Britain, endanger both my own and my family's life, I thought it wise to join the Consular party. Thereupon the British Consul sent a telegram and a letter to the U.S. Consul in Harput, Mr. Louis Davies [sic, Leslie Davis], strongly recommending you, and placing you all under his protection.

On Saturday, the 31st of October 1914 at about midday, a cipher telegram arrived from the British Embassy at Constantinople, stating that Turkey had finally joined the Central Powers and declared war against the Entente, giving the necessary orders for the immediate departure of the Consular Staff. Within two hours of the receipt of the telegram we had, as a precautionary measure, destroyed – mostly by burning – all the most important documents of the Consulate, after which we called on the Vali and informed him of the instructions received. The poor man looked thunderstruck and could not believe what we had told him, saying that to his mind the telegram appeared to be a false one, and that Turkey was not so mad as to commit suicide at the present moment, for to declare was against England meant sure and certain death for Turkey, a statement which he had often on other occasions repeated. While we were still with him, a telegram came from the Vali of Bagdad, saying that the British, French and Russian representatives in that place had asked for their passports because they had been informed by their respective Governments that Turkey had joined the Central Powers and declared war against the Allies, and that since he (the Vali of Bagdad) had not received any instruction from Constantinople, he would feel greatly obliged if Hamid Bey could possibly enlighten him on this subject. The British Consul then told Hamid Bey that this telegram proved that the directors of the Committee of Union and Progress, Talaat, Enver and Jemal Pashas, were masters of the situation in Constantinople, and that they had arranged on their own account without taking the least trouble to consult the provinces. By sunset that same day the Vali very kindly sent the usual "Bouyouroultou" (travelling permit) to the Consulate.

The piece of news spread at once throughout the city like a flash of lightning. Nothing can describe the sorrow of the Christian population when they heard that the British Consulate, which they used to consider as their last place of refuge and protection, would now be shut, and that the British Consul, on whom they had placed their last hopes, would leave them soon. The Muslim population also felt embarrassed and could not adequately grasp the importance of the critical events which so rapidly succeeded each other.

On Sunday the 1st of November we left Diyarbekir before daybreak in four carts. The party consisted of the following: the British Consul, Mr. Monck-Mason, Mrs. Monck-Mason and baby [girl] in arms, [Wahidiye] their Maronite servant girl, and myself. On the evening of the first night we reached Kainakh, of the second day Kara-Jouroun, and of the third day Ourfa, thus covering a distance of (150 miles) in 30 hours — a distance usually covered in six days, in only three.

The Mutessarif of Ourfa, Mumtaz Bey, refused to give us the usual escort for our protection. He behaved in a most unceremonious way, insisted on my not going with the Consul and, in brief, did his best to keep us back. But through the assistance of the Police Commissioner of Ourfa, who was a very polite and kind hearted man, I succeeded in settling my case, and so, on November 4th we left Ourfa, reaching Suruj in the afternoon. At midnight I was called out of my bed by the officer, a lad of 20-24 years of age, in charge of the Recruiting Office of this village, and was told that general telegraphic orders had been sent from Constantinople throughout Turkey not to allow any foreign subject, who intended to leave Turkey, to proceed on his way, and to stop all those who had already started wherever this order found them. Mr. Monck-Mason immediately despatched three "urgent" telegrams (paying three times the regular fare) to the U.S. Ambassador in Constantinople, to the U.S. Consul of Aleppo, and to the Vali of Diyarbekir, asking them to interfere on our behalf so that permission might be granted for our reaching at least the sea-coast. Suspecting possible detention of our telegrams at the Telegraph Office, we paid large sums of money and sent during that same night a confidential messenger to the U.S. Consul Mr.

Jackson at Aleppo and another to the U.S. Consul and Missionary, Mr. Leslie, at Ourfa, with letters giving full details of our unpleasant situation

On Friday the 6th November a telegram came from Mr. Jackson, and a few hours later a second one from the U.S. Ambassador, saying that orders had been sent by the Minister of the Interior to allow us to proceed to Aleppo. On Sunday the 8th November after many difficulties we left Suruj for the nearest railway station, from which we took the train and reached Aleppo, one hour after sunset. As soon as we arrived there and took our rooms at the Hotel Baron, both the U.S and Italian Consuls called and inquired after us. On the following day Mr. Jackson had, by a skillful trick, our Bouyuroultus visaed by the Governor of Aleppo, thus enabling us to go to Beyrout. In the meantime, the story reached our ears that under such similar arrangements the British Consul of Aleppo and other places left from Aleppo by train for Beyrout, but they were instead taken to and imprisoned at Damascus. We therefore applied separately to the Director of the Police of Aleppo – a relation of Vahaj Bey who proved to you of such great value and assistance in Harput – and he made a nice arrangement for us, detailing a police commissioner to accompany us as far as Ryak, the station where we had to change trains, and see that we were safely taken on the Beyrout and not on the Damascus train. Thus at midnight of Tuesday the 10th of November we arrived at Beyrout, at the station of which we were met by the U.S. Consul, Mr. Cheesbery, who took us to Hotel Basul.

On the morning of the 11th November I desired to visit the director of the Post and Telegraph Office, Galib Bey, an old acquaintance of mine from Diyarbekir, to whom I had rendered good services during the reign of Abdul Hamid. Three times I was forbidden by the sentry who had been placed at our doors to leave the hotel premises, but on my fourth attempt I found that the sentry had changed and the new one on duty was a Kurd who knew Kurdish and not a single word of Turkish. I spoke to him in a sweet manner and in his own tongue, put a little "baksheesh" in hand, and I safely slipped away. Galib Bey was more than surprised to see me and wondered how I had managed to reach Beyrout safe and sound. He told me that the Turkish Authorities of Constantinople had condemned me to death, and that strict orders had been sent to every place in Turkey for my arrest. He also gave me the news that our houses, vineyards, and all of our property in Diyarbekir, as well as all our estate in Farkin and elsewhere had already been confiscated. Mindful of our friendship, he told me that he had not, up to that moment, delivered the telegram about me to the Governor of Beyrout, and that he would not hand it to him until he knew that I had safely gone beyond their reach. He furthermore was good enough to send from me a telegraphic Money Order for the sum of six Turkish pounds to the U.S. Consul in Harpout for you. He also exerted all his influence so that the Director of the Police would allow me to leave the hotel and stay wherever I pleased without his keeping track of my whereabouts. The photographer Mr. Samuel Sarafian kindly offered his hospitality to me and so by remaining in his home I evaded all possible dangers on the part of the local authorities.

On the 14th November the declaration of Holy War by the Khalif of the Muslim world (the Sultan of Turkey) was announced with great dignity and ceremonies in Beyrout.

On the 15th of November the dragomans of the French and Russian Consulates in Beirut were suddenly arrested and sent under escort to Konia. The Honorary Dragoman of the British Consulate at Beyrout, Spiro Bey Shuker was exiled to Damascus. On the same day, the Governor of the Independent Province of Lebanon Hovannes Pasha Kouyoumjian (Armenian by nationality) with his staff, and the Maronite Patriarch were arrested and sent to Damascus.

Monday the 16th November was our day of deliverance. Through the influential assistance of the U.S. Consul General, permission was secured for our departure and in the forenoon accompanied by the U.S. Vice-Consul, Mr. Cheesbery, the President of the Syrian Protestant College Dr. Howard Daniel Bliss, Dr. Graham and others we were taken together with baggage etc. by the small American launch on board one of the Italian Maritime Service Company steamers. By eight o'clock that night our boat, which was more than crowed with a large number of passengers all flying from present and prospective Turkish terrors, pulled up its anchor. The crowd on board was so large that although I had a 2nd class ticket, only a chair was apportioned to me on the deck of the steamer, and on this chair I had to sit all day long motionless and sleep as best as I could during the night. The weather was exceedingly rough that night and heavy rain was pouring, so that I got wet through.

On the morning of the 17th we touched Haifa, and in the evening of that same day Jaffa. New crowds of passengers came from both these ports. Drawing rooms, halls, decks, corridors, every space available was crammed and the boat was groaning under the tremendous weight of so many passengers. Many could not find a place to sit and remained standing until the end of the voyage. Though traveling under such disadvantages and difficulties, there were no complaints and everybody was glad that he had actually left behind the place they called Turkey. The weather continued rough and stormy throughout the whole day.

We reached Port-Said, this important sea port at the entrance of the famous Suez Canal, on the morning of Wednesday the 18th of November. After a lengthy and minute cross-examination which lasted for fully five hours the Consular party was allowed to land at Port Said, while the rest of the passengers were taken to Alexandria. We reached Cairo safe and sound on the following day, the 19th of November, on which occasion I offered most hearty thanks to our Heavenly Father for having brought me out of Turkey. But my whole heart and soul were bleeding at the realization that I had been unable to take you and our six dear ones with me to this safe place. The only thing I could then do was to pray for your safety and to commit you to the care of Him Whose eye never sleepeth, and to provide you with as much financial support as I could.

I thank God that your escape did so miraculously later take place, and that you succeeded in going away from Turkey. I know too well that the glory of having saved our six children belongs wholly to you, and I know that God, to whom you surrendered yourself with your faith, took you by the hand as the heroine in "Pilgrim's Progress" and led you out of the Valley of the Shadow of Death. Thanks be again to God for having delivered you and our six children from all Turkish toils and Russian horrors.

Having now come to the end of my own personal experiences I will give you a chronological summary of what took place in Diyarbekir during those red-blood days, when the Turanian Government of the Committee of Union and Progress in Constantinople, having lost all human sense undertook, at the inspiration and instructions that proceeded from their worthy allies, the Germans, these vandals of the present age, to exterminate a whole race by killing, massacring, annihilating and even crucifying the Armenian everywhere.

[PART II]

An Assassin Governor
— Dr. Reshid Bey

Naturally a strong, just and honest Vali like Hamid Bey could not for a long time remain in such a position. As soon as the political atmosphere became totally dark, and the Committee of Union and Progress saw that he was an obstacle to their plans, he was recalled to Constantinople and Dr. Reshid Bey, a real assassin, a Circassian by birth, and a former Governor of Mosul was appointed in his place. Dr. Reshid Bey is well known too as the Mutessarif of Karasi. He arrived at Diyarbekir on the 28th of March 1915 and brought with him the following hangmen: Colonel Rushdi Bey (Circassian) as the commandant of the gendarmerie, Bedreddin Bey as his Chief Secretary, Major Shakir Bey (a Circassian) as his aide-de-camps, and approximately 50 more Circassian brigands [*chetejis*], who were shortly dressed in gendarmes' uniform and became in the hands of the Committee of Union and Progress of Diyarbekir the ablest tools for the destruction of Armenians.

Deputy Feizy Bey and His Bonus of 150,000 Piasters to the Committee of Union and Progress

[Ottoman Parliamentary] Deputy Feizy Bey was at that period exceedingly occupied. He had all possible means and opportunities within his reach. He proved himself the worthy son of the famous Chief of Robbers and Brigands, Pirinji Zade Arif Effendi, who during the Armenian massacres of 1895 put himself at the head of his Kurdish bands and directed all their movements and plans throughout those days of massacre both in the town and in the vilayet of Diyarbekir. As a recompense for his faithful service he was, after the declaration of the Turkish constitution, elected Deputy of Diyarbekir to the 1st Parliament.

When Feizy some time ago was in Constantinople, he carried on active and extensive negotiations with the most important leaders of the Committee on Union and Progress, promising them the sum of

15,000,000 piasters for an organised Armenian massacre. He even gave them a written promise to the effect, and thus succeeded in extracting their consent for the so much desired massacres of the Armenians. When subsequently the order for the massacres were so successfully executed, he collected the above stated enormous sum from the confiscated and abandoned property of the Armenians and faithfully remitted it to the Chief Executioners at Constantinople thus fully redeeming his promise.

As soon as the necessary final instructions arrived from the capital, Feizy, Reshid, Bedreddin and Rushdi drew up the well known plan for the systematic extermination of the Armenians of the vilayet. To back them up in this enterprise they had the unscrupulous Guevranli Zade Memdouh Bey, who had been exiled by the former Governor Hamid Bey to Adana, recalled and reappointed to his former position of Police Commissioner. This pronounced enemy of the Armenians could not but become the best and most effective person associated in this hellish work of destruction, devastation and extermination.

The Militia

During the month of April 1915 the Committee of Union and Progress of Diyarbekir received orders from the Vali, Dr. Reshid Bey to organise a militia. Thereupon they picked out from both the town and village of Diyarbekir the worst specimens of thieves, brigands, murders, deserters etc. and formed them into eleven battalions to which they shamelessly gave the name militia [*tabur cheteji*]. These units were naturally nothing more or less than a new revised edition of the Janissaries. The most fanatical and merciless members of the Committee of Union and Progress were appointed at the head of this militia. Their names are as follows: Jemil Pasha Zade Mustafa Bey, appointed with the rank of Colonel as Commander in Chief of the Militia. He and his brother Kassim had already won a very bad reputation for their scandalous conduct during the 1895 massacres. The whole Jemil Pasha family was renowned for its cruelty and inhumanity.

Yassin Zade Shevki Bey, (a very influential member of the Diyarbekir Committee of Union of Progress) appointed as Assistant to the above with the rank of Major.

The following professional murderers were appointed with the rank of Captain at the head of each of the eleven battalions of the militia.

1. Pirinchi Zade Sidki Effendi. [From Diyarbekir]
2. Delel Zade Emin Bey. [From Diyarbekir]
3. Sheyh Zade Kadri Bey. [From Diyarbekir]
4. Zaza Zade Mohammed Bey. [From Diyarbekir]
5. Mosulli Yahiya Bey. [Lives in Diyarbekir]
6. Molla Yahiya Bey. [From Diyarbekir]
7. Mukhtar Zade Oturakji Salih. [From Diyarbekir]
8. Direkji Tahir. [From Diyarbekir]
9. Ali Hato Zade Salih [From Diyarbekir]
10. Haji Bakir. [From Diyarbekir]
11. Kurd Kassab Hecho.* [From Diyarbekir]
    Kurd Kassab Sheykho.* [From Diyarbekir]

* Both of them in charge of the 11th Battalion.

The name of *Kassab Taburu* (the Butcher's Battalion) was given to the 11th Battalion, and the last two named "Kassab" (butchers) were given charge of it. Each of these 12 Captains had 300 men directly under his orders, whom they could increase to as many as the requirements and the exigencies of the situation required from what they called their "reserve."* The special task given to the Butchers' Battalion was to spread at once terror throughout the country by all the loyal and disloyal means [sic], one of which was to seize men by the throat, strangle them, cut them into pieces and then hang them in their own butchers' shop!

Fifty famous murderers were appointed as Sergeants and 500 more with the same qualifications as Corporals of this infamous militia. The names of the officers, N.C.O.'s and men of the militia were officially registered in the government books as if serving with the regular Turkish Army.

---

* The Armenian original states that each of the ten *taburs* consisted of 500 people, while the eleventh *kasab tabur* had 150 people in it. —A.S.

Persons Responsible for the Armenian Massacres in the Vilayet of Diyarbekir

Chief and above all the so-called militia, this gang of blood-red criminals were responsible for the systematic implementation of the atrocities and massacres throughout the vilayet of Diyarbekir. The following officials of the civilian government share equally the responsibility with the fourteen leaders of the militia, and with the Chief Executioners, Enver, Talaat, and Jemal.

1. The Governor of Diyarbekir, Dr. Reshid Bey (Circassian).
2. The Chief Secretary of the Province, Bedreddin. He was later appointed to the position of Mutessarif of Mardin, and there he stirred up and carried out to his perfect satisfaction new Armenian massacres.[*]
3. The Commandant of Gendarmerie Colonel Rushdi Bey (Circassian).
4. The Aide-de-Camp of Dr. Rushdi Bey, Major Shakir (Circassian).
5. Deputy Pirinci Zade Feizy Bey. [From Diyarbekir]
6. The Director of the Police, Jemil Bey (Circassian)
7. Deputy Zilfi Zade Zilfi Bey. From Diyarbekir]
8. The Chief Police Commissioner, Resul Bey (Albanian). [From Diyarbekir]
9. The Police Commissioner, Guevranli Zade Memdouh Bey. [From Diyarbekir]
10. The Inspector of Committee of Union and Progress Jirlis Agha Zade Kior Yussuf.
11. The Chief of Committee of Union and Progress Attar Hakki Effendi. [From Diyarbekir]
12. Mufti Zade Sherif Bey.
13. Captain Vali Baba Veli[†] (Boneli) member of the Committee of Union and Progress.

---

[*] The Armenian text states that these massacres were carried out with the help of the eshrefs —A.S.

[†] The English translation has an illegible handwritten entry here. —A.S.

14. Zilfi Zade Adil Bey.
15. Abdul Kadir Effendi Zade Kemal Effendi.[*]

The Superior Council [*Mejlisi Ali*]

The persons whose names have just been given together with the fourteen leaders of the militia incorporated themselves into a group which they called "the Superior Council". The Vali Dr. Reshid Bey was the president of this Council and Deputy Feizy was the Vice-President. They met regularly and set down in full details the plans and programmes for the massacres which were to be carried out against the Armenians. They were efficiently assisted in the systematic execution of their satanical plans by the Militia, the Circassian bands of robbers, and the Kurdish population.[†]

Armenian Soldiers Under the Crescent

On the 23rd of July 1908 the Turkish Constitution was declared. The despotic power of the Red Sultan Abdul Hamid was broken to pieces and the very foundations of his throne were shaken. The people of Turkey tasted on that occasion the life giving spirits of Liberty, Justice, Equality and Brotherhood, and actually believed that oppression, misrule, tyranny and persecution had been done away with, and that days of blessing and prosperity were most assuredly in store for everybody. Even Europe was amazed at Turkey's sudden and magical transformation. The Armenians were more than dazzled and in the excitement and frenzy of the moment forgot and forgave their old enemies, and in a spirit of brotherhood embraced and kissed their hangmen of yesterday.

When the first Turkish Parliament met, the Armenian deputies under the leadership of their most-prized deputy Krikor Zohrab Effendi, put forward very strong appeals to have all the non-Muslim youths thereafter serve in the Turkish Army, and they finally succeeded in obtaining the sanction of the Chamber. The whole Armenian nation gladly accepted to

---

[*] The Armenian text states: Kemal Effendi *istinab katibi* Abdul Kadir's son, one of the leaders of the Committee of Union and Progress —A.S.
[†] The Armenian original describes the latter as Circassian *chetejis* and Circassians living in the province. —A.S.

give their sons to serve the interests of the country to which they belonged and the government whose liberated subjects they then thought they were. Thanks to their intuitive talents and their higher education the Armenians made speedy progress and displayed great ability and capacity in their military career. One of the Fourth Army Generals said once in the course of a conversation that the Armenian soldiers learned in a month what the Turks required a year and the Kurds two years to learn. Another General of the Ottoman Army made on another occasion the following most significant remark: "I prefer to be in charge of an Armenian Regiment than in charge of a Kurdish Army."

Labour Battalions

This illusion on the part of Armenians continued up to the end of 1914, when orders were sent from the Ministry of War to take away all arms from Armenian soldiers and transfer them into the *Amelay Taburlari* (Labour Battalions). They then woke from their dream and realised the falsity of the situation. They were taken into distant and mountainous regions to break stone and to construct roads and fortifications just like ordinary workmen, or like criminals condemned to hard labour, away from all Armenians and civilisation and under the command of most tyrannical officers.

Thus very soon Diyarbekir like all other towns with a majority of Armenian population* saw her sons go away and in most cases never to come back again – or lost all possible communication and relation with them. One could then see at home only boys below 17 and old men above 50. The majority of those men over 50 years old were priests and teachers, merchants, farmers, artisans, etc. and such others as the authorities could not very well then take without injury to their own interests. As an exception a few young men could be seen, but these had paid a threefold exemption fee.

* The Armenian text states "centres with large Armenian populations." The English translation is clearly in error. —A.S.

The Secret Trip

On Monday the 19th April 1915 Deputy Feizy Bey, acting on instructions from the Superior Council (mentioned above) left on a special mission to Jeziret-el-Oumer, a village on the bank of the Tigris. Both on his way to and from this place he skilfully carried on propaganda among the Kurdish and the other Muslim population in general, advising, exciting and stirring them up to perform their religious duties and obligations, the most important of which was to massacre and annihilate the infidels, and especially the Armenians, sparing neither old nor young, neither man nor woman, with the exception of beautiful women and girls, who could embellish their harems. The Sheikhs and Hojas undersigned his words by quoting the following verses from the Koran, which is read every Friday in mosque. "Allahuma yetim atfalehem ve rammel nisaahum, ve ijalhum zanimetten lel Muslimin" (O God make their (the infidels) children orphans, their wives widows, and give their property to the Muslims.) The also quoted the following common proverb amongst Muslims: "The property, the life and the honour (wife) of the infidels is a rightful prey to the Muslim."

To give greater weight to his words Feizy assured them that the Allies of Turkey, Germany and Austria, had both given their consent and permission for this, and that they would not interfere with them in any way.

On his way back Feizy stopped at Shkefta, a Kurdish village on the Tigris belonging to the Rama tribe, and there he was entertained by the widow of the late Chief of the Tribe, Perikhan. At Feizy's request she sent her son Amero, one of those savage Kurdish brigands who had been condemned to death at least a dozen times by the Turkish government, and the order for whose arrest, whether alive or dead [*heyiten ve meyiten*], had been just as many times issues. When he ventured to come down from his refuge on the mountains, Feizy told him that an Imperial pardon had been granted him, and that in return for this he would do certain things which would prove that he was worthy of the Padishah's pardon and of the prophet's blessing. He would kill all Armenians who were shortly to be deported on rafts from Diyarbekir to Mosul!

Thus Feizy after having given in a like manner instructions to all the Kurdish, Arab and Circassian chiefs, sheikhs, notables and their people in general for the extermination of the Armenians on their way to exile, and after having completed all the necessary satantical arrangements for the success of his infernal scheme, he went back to Diyarbekir, where, as expected, his associates had put everything in perfect order.

Arrest and Imprisonment

The arrest of the Armenians in the city of Diyarbekir was started on Friday the 16th April 1915. During the night all the Armenian quarters were surrounded by the Muslims, while the streets of the quarters, the roofs, doors and every opening of the houses were guarded by soldiers, gendarmes, civil and military police, Circassian irregulars, and Militia men. A thorough search followed in every house under the pretext of looking for deserters. In reality all sorts of arms, including sporting rifles and ordinary knives were seized, and more than 300 young men were put under arrest. Instead of taking them to the military recruiting offices, as one would naturally have expected, they cast them into the regular Turkish prisons, as regular malefactors.

On Monday the 19th April 1915 the Authorities arrested all the members of the different local Armenian philanthropic committees and Associations, such as the Committee of Notables, the Religious, Educational, Financial, Benevolent and other such establishments for the administration of the local affairs of the Armenian Community. After a typical and meaningless interrogation all of them were imprisoned.

On Wednesday the 21st 1915 the heads of the Armenian Political Committees, that is the Tashnag, Hunchag, and Democratic [Ramgavars] were also arrested and imprisoned.

The turn of the most influential and important members of the Armenian Community came on 1st of May[*] when without any distinction Government employees, lawyers, men of intellect and education, merchants, bankers, landowners, manufactures, engineers and

---

[*] The Armenian original gives the date of 11th May, not the 1st of May. —A.S.

a great part of the well-to-do artisans were caught and put into prison. A room with a seating capacity for 50 men was crowded with 300 to 350 men. These men were taken away all of a sudden from their families and home comforts, and at the same time deprived of all possible means of communication with the outside world. They were in a most miserable conditions within the walls of those modern "black holes." It is beyond human power and descriptive imagination of any man to represent the filth, the awful smell, the stinking air, the suffocating atmosphere of those wretched dungeons, where these poor, innocent Armenians, who but a few moments ago were the leaders of their Community, were so cruelly thrown.

The clergy was not spared and the following men were arrested and imprisoned: the Armenian Bishop, Rev. Mugerdich Chlghadian with his nine prelates, the Armenian Catholic Archbishop Rev. Andreas Chelebian with his three priests, and the Armenian Protestant Pastor Rev. Hagop Andonian.[*]

By the end of May the total of Armenians who had been put in prison amounted to 980 people.[†]

An Important Meeting of the Armenians

When the above mentioned arrests and imprisonment began in April, the Armenian political committees

Armenian Catholic Archbishop of Diyarbekir "Kerabaidzar" Andreas Chelebian

---

* These three men were the leaders of their respective communities. The Armenian text also states that Chlghadian was the son of Der Mugerdich Kahana Chlghadian of Tadvan. —A.S.

† The actual date given in the Armenian text is 27 May. —A.S.

AGBU Committee, Diyarbekir, 1913. (*left to right*) Misag Eff. Shirigjian, merchant and landowner; Sdepan Eff. Matosian, merchant; Bishop Zaven Der Yeghiayan, later Patriarch of Constantinople; Haroutiun Eff. Boyajian, silk factory owner; Haroutiun Eff. Kasabian, dragoman of the French Consulate; Dikran Eff. Ilvanian, dragoman of vilayet.

thought it necessary to call a meeting to discuss the situation. Each of the three committees Tashang, Hunchag and Democratic, sent its own president and three of its leading members to the house of the Armenian bishop, Rev. Mugerdich Chlghadian, where under his presidency the meeting was opened. As soon, however, as these men began to discuss the situation they realised that this question effected the whole of the Armenian community and therefore it ought to have been brought before a general meeting with all the representatives of the other committees of the Armenian community present. Accordingly, they sent for representatives from the committees of notables, religious, educational, financial, benevolent organisations, etc. as well as from the Armenian-Catholic and Armenian-Protestant Communities.

The order of the day was very simple: Could the Armenians of Diyarbekir under their present strait circumstances and means present any resistance and defend themselves against the aggressors, or should they believe the promises of the Turks and give up their arms? The "pros" and "cons" were heard and a very long discussion followed, lasting for the whole day and the ensuing night. The presidents of the three political committees, the French dragoman and Pro-Consul Haji Haroutiun Kassabian, Messrs. Diran, Attalah and Jirjis Kazazian (the last being a member of the Turkish Provincial Council [*Mejlisi idare*]), the Dragoman of the Vilayet Dikran Ilvanian, Stepan Mattossian, the Donjians, the Lawyer Kiragoz Yenofkian with the Armenian Bishop as their leader insisted that the Armenians ought to defend themselves, their women, children and property, as well as their honour [*namous*] to the last man and bullet, and sell their skin at as high a price as possible; that, judging from past experience, they ought not to have any confidence in the treacherous [*jellad*] Turkish government, nor believe the false promises of the rogues of the Committee of Union and Progress.

The other party consisting of Emish Kazazian, the Torpajian brothers, the Yeghenian [sic, Yeganian] brothers, the Handanian [sic, Khandenian] brothers and others with Khachadour Dikranian as their head insisted on exactly the opposite policy. They argued that the means at the disposal of Armenians were insufficient, that under present conditions and arrangements they might hold out for a month at the most, after which the worst revenge from the Turks would befall them etc. Khachadour Dikranian, who was a member of the Turkish Provincial Council too, relying on his power and authority, made a most amazing statement in support of the policy which he thought the Armenians ought to pursue. He emphatically and categorically declared that he could immediately send the Bishop into exile, and would by Government means arrest and exile all those who unwisely and imprudently advised resistance and defence. Everyone was shocked at his threatening words, and the whole case for self-defence was dropped. The lamentable results of the adopted policy of submission were soon made manifest, and even the supporters of this policy and their families did not escape the cruel fate that the Turks had fore-ordained for every Armenian.

Tortures in Prison – Death from Flogging

Deputy Feizy and Vali Dr. Reshid Bey, the Assassins, together with the clique of the Committee of Union and Progress displayed such great inventive faculties in the way and manner of torturing the Armenians that they foreshadowed all the cruelest and most brutal ancient and dark-age tyrants.

The following list of the persons who were the first to suffer in their hands and the way in which they were tortured can give but a faint idea of their terrible inventions.

Members of the Tashang Committees:

Mihran Bastajian, one of the committee leaders. A very brilliant young man. Graduate from the American Euphrates College.

Giragos Ohanessian.

Dikran Chakijian.

Kassab Vaho.

Hagop Boghos, the blacksmith.

Police Hovan, the silversmith.

Member of the Hunchag Committees:

Deputy Stepan Chirajian, one of the Committee leaders. He had a complete knowledge of the Turkish language and was very clever and devoted to his nation.

Garabed Chirajian, son of the above. Mudir of the village Habab. Educated in Euphrates College.

Khosrov Chirajian, brother of the above. Secretary of the Court of Appeal. Graduate of Euphrates College.

Members of the Democratic Committee:

Hagop Oghasarian. A graduate of Euphrates College. He had been for many years in the United States, but had come back in 1910.

Dikran Ilvanian. Dragoman of the Vilayet. Secretary of the Armenian Benevolent Society [AGBU]. Graduate of the American Central Turkey College. A very energetic young man.

Stepan Mattossian. Member of the Armenian National Assembly of Notables, and Inspector of the Armenian Benevolent Committee [AGBU]. A wealthy merchant and an agent for Standard Oil Company.

Misak Shirigjian, member of the Municipal Council, [member of the AGBU], merchant, agent of the Signer Company. Haji Kassabian, Dragoman and Pro-Consul of the French Consulate in Diyarbekir.

The above named, a good many of the Armenian higher class, and a large number of those who had already been imprisoned were subjected to all possible sorts of flogging and tortures. Hagop Bozo and some of his associates were shoed and compelled to run like horses. They drove red-hot horse shoes in the breast of Mihran Bastajian and his associates. They forced some others to put their heads under big presses, and then by turning the handles they crushed the heads to pieces. Others they mutilated or pulled their nails out with pincers. In other more slow cases, they first pulled the nails with pincers, then pressed the fingers under a heavy press, after which they cut the fingers one by one. Darakji Hagop was operated on his private parts. Others were flayed alive. Some were taken to the slaughter house, killed and their flesh distributed as if for sale to the butchers! Police Ohan and his friends were crucified and had long nails driven through their hands and feet... Such were the tortures and excruciating pain and agony of the victims so that the survivors offered all that they had left them. They begged and implored their tormentors not for their lives, but for a rifle shot that would put a quick end to their earthly existence. But their requests were met with scorn and were boastfully rejected. The hopeless sighs and the desperate cries of the tyrannised victims were rending the skies, while the ferocious and heartless Turks and Kurds, unmoved by the scene of suffering around them, thoroughly enjoyed the situation and rejoiced at their accomplishments.

The sufferings, the pains, the tortures of the Armenian Bishop Mugerdich Chlghadian are beyond any human description, imagination, and constitute by themselves the crowning feature of Turkish brutality and monstrosity. This martyr bishop was first the subject to the most outrageous insults and was dragged though the city street for a public show, while the sheikhs, the dervishes etc. with the musical instruments headed this disreputable procession. He was then led to the Mosque of the Governorate and there, in the presence of the civil and military authorities and a large crowd of Muslim fanatics, they poured petroleum over his clothes and set fire to them, burning him almost to death. At the point of expiration they put out the flames and threw him into the stables of the hospital of the municipality, there to die in the midst of the most terrible pains.

Other members of the clergy met with similar tortures and death.

A Good Samaritan

Throughout all these tortures the eyes of all Armenians who were so shamefully treated were turned towards one, only one, human being who could possibly come to their assistance, the American missionary Dr. Smith. This self-sacrificing man took no notice whatever of hard work and labour but did all that was humanly possible to relieve, help, comfort and cheer the dying Armenians. Drugs and medicine to those who had been through tortures, wounds and bruises, bread and even fruits to the hungry, money to the needy, all these he freely and gladly offered to all who needed them. He ministered to their last needs, prayed with the dying, closed the eyes of the dead. (The corpses of the dead were ultimately taken by the Turks and without any religious ceremony thrown into the drains.) This doctor was generally called by the poor miserable sufferers "the good doctor." He could not unfortunately escape the eye and notice of the Assassin-in-Chief, Dr. Reshid Bey, nor could he continue his noble work without the Turks putting an end to it.

When he (the American doctor) heard that the Martyr Bishop had been thrown half burnt and still in a semi-conscious state into the stables of the hospital of the municipality, he ran on the spot to see if he could be of any assistance to him. He found him in a totally unrecognisable condition, writhing in the midst of terrible pains with a black piece of dirty rag thrown over him, and past all hopes of life. When the Vali was informed of this he immediately had him brought before him and insulted him in the most unceremonious way, forbidding him after that incident to enter the premises of the Government Hospital or any other place where he could be of help to Armenians. Dr. Smith, realising that his stay in Diyarbekir was useless after that, decided to send first his family to join the other Americans in Harput and then go there himself too.

On leaving her house Mrs. Smith was arrested by the policemen and subjected by them to a most trying and minute examination as a result of which a brief report addressed by her husband to the U.S. Consul and the American missionaries in Harput was found under her arm pit. The Vali then ordered a general and most thorough search of Dr. Smith's house.

When the British Consul, Mr. Monck-Mason, went away from Diyarbekir, he made some valuable documents into a parcel, which he officially sealed and at night handed over to Dr. Smith with the requested that on the first presented opportunity he would forward it to the U.S. Consulate in Harput. This parcel had not been sent to Harput up to that time and was discovered and seized by Dr. Reshid's men. Naturally, this discovery provoked the Vali more than anything else, and he immediately sent Dr. Smith and family away from Diyarbekir. In this way the Armenians of Diyarbekir were deprived of their good, sympathetic, brave, self-sacrificing friend, and lost their only last hope that they had maintained up to then.

A Kurdish Brigand

On an invitation from Vali, the chief of the Rama tribe Shkeftanlu Amero, came to Diyarbekir and was directly received by him. Amero was of a short stature, darkish, with small-pox scars on his face. He wore a big turban on his head around which hung many coloured silk insignias to show that he was a Kurdish chief. He also wore a black short tunic (local made), long breeches, and red shoes. He presented the picture of a portable armoury, being armed with a Mauser rifle, two revolvers, a sword, a dagger, a *yataghan*, and carrying with him an enormous amount of bullets and cartridges.

This born brigand, who had never seen any education, nor civilisation, who had spent his whole life on the mountains living in their cavities and woods, who had known no other work than robbing and killing, who had been at least ten times condemned to death by the

Turkish authorities for his atrocities, this very same man who was on that occasion officially received and welcomed by Deputy Feizy Bey and Colonel Rushdi Bey (gendarmerie commanding officer), was taken on a carriage and with military honours to the Governor's Palace. The Vali received him very graciously and told him the following, which being said in Turkish had to be translated by Feizy into Kurdish for the sake of the great guest:

"My son Amero. Within the next few days my aide-de-camp Major Shakir Bey will take a party of about 700 wealthy Armenians on river rafts down to Mosul. Will you kindly see that when this party reaches your village of Shkefta your own men, following the instructions and directions which will be given by Major Shakir Bey, attack and wholly destroy them? If I hear that even one of them has escaped, you will be held personally responsible, but if this is done well I will see that you get the suitable medal from the Sultan in appreciation of the valuable services which you will have rendered us. I will also give the reward which you deserve."

Amero expressed his gratitude and thanks for the honour entrusted to him and assured them of its successful outcome by saying thanks in Kurdish: "Ser saro min, ser chavo min" (upon my head, and upon my eyes). He was then given full details and instructions by the Vali Dr. Reshid Bey and Deputy Feizy and left on a raft for his village taking with him two cartloads of rope which were presented to him by the Requisitioning Commission.

The Martyrs of the Valley of Bezwan

At the Vali's requests a Court of Inquiry was established under the presidency of Deputy Feizy to look into the case, examine and pass sentence on the Armenians who were still alive in prison. Feizy then inspected them superficially and made a list of the most important and influential persons. It is interesting to note that Feizy who, shortly before these events began, used to stand with crossed hands and full respect in the presence of not a few of the Armenians who were now sighing in prison, was the Chief Judge in front of whom these unhappy men would come with awe to hear him pass sentence!

On Sunday, the 30th May these 635 men, who constituted the "elite" of the city and the vilayet of Diyarbekir were put on 23 rafts [*keleks*] and under strong escorts made up of militia men and Circassians whose leader was Major Shakir Bey started for their fatal trip to Mosul.

On Wednesday the 9th June they arrived at Shkefta. Before reaching that place, however, Major Shakir Bey has a secret meeting with Amero in which all the final details of the massacre were settled. The following incident also occurred: While the rafts were sailing down the Tigris quite a large party of brigands appeared on the bank and fired two shots at the rafts thereby presumably ordering them to stop. Immediately Shakir Bey landed a force to chase them away. They soon returned and reported that three of the brigands had been killed while the rest fled to the mountains. In reality no one had been killed and this trick was part of the tragedy that was to follow. This little incident was brought in to make the Armenians trust their hangmen.

After this incident Shakir Bey was on the same raft with the rich Armenians Emish, Jirjis and Diran Kazazian, Khachadour Dikranian and a dozen or so of other rich Armenians. He called them together and pointed out that since the part of the country that they were passing through was full of Kurdish brigands, and consequently very dangerous, it would be wiser and safer if all the exiles who happened to be in possession of any gold handed it to him, so that in case of any emergency he might be able, thanks to the stronger force on his raft, defend it better than anyone else. They believed his argument and in the course of a few minutes the sum of more than 6,000 pounds in gold was placed in Major Shakir's bag.

On arrival at Shkefta [on June 9th] the 635 exiles were landed for a 24 hour rest. Amero at once called on Major Shakir Bey bringing with him some provisions, part of which he also gave to some of the Armenians who in time past had been good to him. In their hearing he said to the Major that he had heard that both banks of the Tigris were occupied by Kurdish brigands, whose plan was to attack the rafts, kill the exiles and rob them of all their belongings. It would therefore be advisable, since the Major and the Armenians were his friends, to stay in his village where they could be safe from all danger and wait further instructions from Diyarbekir. After a short discussion it was decided to accept his offer, and so beginning with the passengers of the Major's raft, they were led out in groups of six to be divided comfortably among the native families, under Amero's personal supervision. As soon as the first group of six unsuspiciously reached the village, they were seized upon by Amero's men, stripped of their clothes, firmly bound with ropes and carried to the Bezwan. In this manner the whole party of 635 exiles were, in groups of six, led out, robbed, bound with ropes and carried to this valley.

The slopes and heights of the mountains on both sides of the valley were occupied by Amero's men.[*] When everything was ready Shakir Bey arrived accompanied by his militia and his Circassian brigands. He gave the signal formerly agreed upon and the most dreadful, cold-blooded, furious massacre started. The firing of the rifles, the buzzing of the shots, the cutting noise of the swords, the clanking of arms in general, the helpless victims' cries of despair filling the whole air. Some of the victims prayed... Others begged for mercy... All in vain... The heavens kept silent... Earth was turned into darkest of Kades... Three hours later everything was quiet in that valley... Perfect silence regained... The corpses of victims were to be seen everywhere. The small stream that passed through the valley for hours flowed red, blood-red... By Major Shakir Bey's orders, some of the Butcher's Battalion men went into the stream to look for possible runaways or survivors. If by any chance they found one they cut his head and then everything was quiet again.

Thus on Wednesday the 9th June 1915 at about sunset, the sun of 635 of the richest, best, leading men of Diyarbekir also set. Their corpses were left a free prey to wild beasts and carnivorous birds.

Fifteen days later the Vali and Feizy invited Amero to go to Diyarbekir and receive the medal which was sent to him by the Sultan, and the reward which they had ready for him. Then Circassians were sent to accompany him on his way to the Governor's Palace. Why? Nobody knows. But those men fell upon Amero and killed him near the sources of Ambar Chai![†]

[*] The Armenian text says the men of the Ramma ashiret. —A.S.

A Special Meeting of the Diyarbekir Muslims and their Decisions

Shortly after the above outrageous crime was committed the Committee of Union and Progress called the leading Muslims of Diyarbekir to a special general meeting under the presidency of Deputy Feizy to take some more ruinous decisions. The following were also present: "Nakib-el-Ashref" Bekir Bey; "Mufti" Ibrahim Effendi; the Notables, Sheikhs, Uleman, Hojas, Pashas, Beys and all the agents of the Committee of Union and Progress.

The order of the day was: Should they massacre all of the 150,000 Armenians of Diyarbekir or only part of them? Was it lawful to kill all the Armenians, men, women, children, both young and old? Did the Koran permit such a wholesome massacre? Could they not spare at least the beautiful women and girls and the babies? All those present in this meeting gave their candid opinion for a general massacre. The Mufti was the only one with... human feelings, and he advised them to spare all children under twelve, because those could easily be converted to Islam. He also asked them to spare the life of the beautiful women and girls and take them into their harems where in due time they also could be converted to the faith of Islam.

This meeting, which was held in the Mosque of Ulu Jami, continued for three days, at the end of which the civil and military authorities were invited to express their opinion and give their advice on the matter. After hearing them, the following decision was unanimously taken: "Spare the beautiful women and girls. Kill the rest." One by one those present in the meeting swore on the Koran to kill their Armenian partners, or neighbours, or friends, or servants, or acquaintances (even babies in arms were not excluded from this general statement), and in case of any Muslim brother attempting to save or help an Armenian to consider him as an enemy of the faith of Islam and kill him as such. They also put this oath in writing which every one of them duly signed. Then this "Death Warrant" was formally handed by Feizy Bey to Dr. Reshid Bey. By this time the thus-far-inconceivable drama of the extermination of Armenians was fully prepared. The official order to raise the curtains was now given too...

---

† The Armenian text says Anbar Chay. —A.S.

Carrying Out the Decision

(A) In Mardin

Armenian Catholic Archbishop of Mardin, Ignatios Maloian.

The Mutessarif Bedreddin, the Police Commissioner Memdouh, and the Armenian Massacres.

Feizy and Reshid Bey, having received from the tyrants of Constantinople the rightful share of thanks and appreciation for faithful services rendered in Diyarbekir in the anti-Armenian movement, grew bolder day by day and finally decided to do the same thing at Mardin. To this effect they chose the Mektoubji Bedreddin and the Police Commissioner Memdouh, who had sworn special capability along these lines in the events of Diyarbekir. Bedreddin was recommended and appointed to the position of Mutesarrif of Madrin, to replace Hilmi Bey, who had been discharged and exiled for having refused to co-operate in the massacres. Memdouh was appointed to the position of the Director of Police. Full authority was given them both and means were placed at their disposal so that not a single Armenian of Mardin, nor one of the Diyarbekir exiles who had already been deported there would escape death.

Without much worry and trouble those two men hit upon an idea that would serve their plans excellently: to cast all the Armenians of Mardin, the exiles from Diyarbekir, and all the others who were being daily deported to southern regions into the terrible underground dungeons which were built at a spot 18 miles to the east of Mardin, thousands of years ago by the Persian king Darius. If these underground holes could not accommodate the whole crowd they would throw the rest into the just as old and just as terrible underground prisons of Ras-ul-Ain.

The following rendered their whole-hearted assistance to the above mentioned two executioners:

Abdul Kadir Pasha Gozo.

Abdul Rahami Kawaz.

Khidir Chelibi (Mayor of Mardin).

Abdul Rezak Chelebi Shahtene.

Mohammed Goubousho.

Abdullah Khidir.

Nejib Effendi (Chief of Taxes Department)

Abdul Kerim Effendi (Director Troops-Department (Transport)) [*sevkiyat muduru*][*]

Soon more than 2,000 Armenian-Catholic and 100 Armenian Protestant families of Mardin were wiped out of existence under the leadership of the above named. The Archbishop Maloyan, the Bishop [Hovhannes] Bodourian, the Protestant pastor Selim Jirjis Hadal, and the rest of the Armenian clergy were one after another put to death.[†] Similar scenes were enacted throughout the province of Mardin.

Dr. Thom, Mr. Andrews, and Miss Fannanga, the American missionaries were sent to exile because they had sympathised with, helped and comforted the victims of the Turks, and because they had accepted from these poor creatures who were being led to death the sum of approximately 7,000 Turkish pounds to transmit to their relatives in the United States. This amount was forcibly taken from the Americans by Bedreddin.[‡] Dr. Thom died on his way to exile and it is strongly

---

[*] The Armenian text also states that "There are still many beautiful Armenian women and girls with each of these men and these captives greatly desire to be freed." —A.S.

[†] The Armenian text also lists amongst the victims Der Mugerdichian Kaliounian and all kahanas, numbering 17 people. —A.S.

[‡] The Armenian text states that the Americans were exiled on 3 October 1915 —A.S.

suspected that he was killed by his Turkish guards. Mr. Andrews, owing to hardship and exhaustion which he experienced, died as soon as he reached his home in America.[*]

(B) In Other Provinces

The authorities in every village of the other provinces of the vilayet of Diyarbekir had received by this time instructions and unlimited authority to co-operate with the militia and the Kurdish population in everything connected with the Armenian deportations. To state it more briefly, they were told to act just as they pleased. First of all the male population was separated and sent to join the Labour Corps. On the way they were robbed of everything they possessed and afterwards killed in the most brutal manner. Then the defenceless and helpless women and children were forcibly dragged out of their homes and under the cudgel of the oppressors were forced into parties and driven to Ras-ul-Ain and Der-Zor, without having been allowed to take with them anything for the trip, except what these "Children of Sorrow" could carry in their small bundles. O God! Who can tell the weeping and the crying, the pain and agony, the horror and affliction of those poor, helpless, comfortless "Children of Sorrow"; of those unprotected husbandless women, fatherless orphans, desolate human beings, who but a few hours ago had been forced under the tyrant's whip to abandon the comforts of their homes, who had lost all they held dear in this world, and were now marched between the lines of fire and sword, between two lines of Godless, inhuman, heartless beasts, towards famine, poverty, pain, dishonour, death? They were marched to unknown destinations, to scorching deserts, to a far distant Golgotha through a way of indescribable and insupportable sufferings, there to meet at least the most horrid crucifixion.

The blood-thirsty Kurds and the militiamen drove these innocent, helpless creatures, who in the twinkling of an eye had been expelled from their cozy nests, in the most merciless and ruthless manner as if they were herds of cattle. Hungry, thirsty, exhausted, feeding on grains, still they

---

[*] The Armenian text ends with the sentence, "In all of Mardin there hardly remained the decimated remnants of 200 families." —A.S.

were driven on and on. The tormentors took away from them all their possessions, their clothing, their very skin, their honour! They left them absolutely nothing. During that most frightful journey they picked out the most beautiful women and girls and forced them to go back to another living death, what they called "the Muslim harems." It is easy to imagine what befell those who were not beautiful, and the old women and children. Dozens of them, nay hundreds, were daily killed and their corpses were scattered on the right and left of this road of Calvary to feed the wild beasts and the fowls of the air.

The gendarmes, the militia, the Kurdish and the Circassians of the land that they were crossing were busy day and night carrying on their ignominious work. Before long all the Armenian villages throughout the vilayet of Diyarbekir had been swept and carried away by this hurricane of inhuman hatred and fanaticism that burst upon them. Finally, after the provinces and the villages, Diyarbekir's own turn came.

(C) Diyarbekir

The decision to deport the whole population of the city of Diyarbekir was taken in July 1915. It was mentioned before how the whole plan of the extermination of Armenians was set out in the special meeting which the Muslims held and how acting on these arrangements Feizy Bey and Dr. Reshid did then send the necessary instructions by men of the Committee of Union and Progress throughout the vilayet, ordering every faithful Muslim to take up arms and annihilate as many Armenians as he could, without distinction either to sex or age, and threatening any one proving unfaithful to this trust with certain death.

When Diyarbekir's turn actually came, the militia Major Yasin Zade Shefki and the Commandant of the Gendarmerie Rushdi Bey (a Circassian) accompanied by a police force and a large number of Circassian bandits went through the Armenian houses daily and put down in a special book the number and names of every family, leaving at the door of each house on going away a militia sentry with orders not to allow any one neither to enter nor to leave the house. As soon as the general registration was complete, the deportations began. Every evening after sunset approximately one hundred houses were emptied and their inhabitants set on the track of exile and death. One day they would start a party on the road to Mardin, and the following day start a party on the road to Kara Baghche. One party was sent to the South and the other to the West, so as never to meet again. These parties were put in charge of merciless, godless and blood-thirsty Circassians and members of the militia, and they were supposed to reach Mardin, Dara, Waweyle, Ras-el Ain and Der-Zor. It is utterly impossible to describe the heart-rending scenes that took place while the above part of the drama was being enacted. Words fails me to tell of how the wild beasts would rush into the houses and in the midst of tears, weepings, groaning, sighs, shrill shrieks and cries of agony and despair seize the women and girls by their hair and pull them out into the dark and gloomy road to exile.

The Armenian Catholic Archbishop Andreas Chelebian, the family of Emsih Sabagh and a number of other rich Armenian Catholic families were led to the Mardin road, but before reaching their destination all of them joined the army of the new Armenian martyrs. The Protestant Pastor Rev. Hagop Andonian with his family, his son-in-law Bedros Mavlian and many other Armenian Protestant families were led to the Kara Baghche road on which they bravely met with death. The wife of Deputy Stepan Chirajian and several other ladies belonging to this party were flayed alive.

The honorary dragoman of the British Consulate Dr. Vosgian Topalian had long ago been exiled to Erzeroum, where he soon succumbed to the hardships and ill treatment that he had been through. His wife and children, who were naturally left alone, were on this occasion asked by the children of their neighbour Osman Effendi to be safely carried away on their own Osman's sons' carts and cattle, to their own village Ak Pinar, a small place on the road to Mardin at a distance of 18 miles from Diyarbekir. This offer was gratefully accepted because the victims trusted on the traditional family friendship which existed between these two families, for let it be mentioned here that Mrs. Toplian's father[*] had been

---

[*] The Armenian text mentions the father's name as Dr. Garabed Pirinjian, leader of the Diyarbekir Protestant community —A.S.

the doctor of Osman Bey's family for 25 years and her husband for eight, which gave a total of 35 years of medical services rendered to this family. Mrs Victoria Mattosian, sister of Mrs. Toplian, with her children was also asked to join the party. At a short distance from Ak Pinar, the older sons asked the two sisters to become their wives, but their audacious proposal was indignantly rejected. They then pressed them at least to accept the Muslim faith, but seeing that their proposals were one after other repulsed with disdain and contempt, they fell upon the defenseless women and children and killed every one of them.

As regards the family of the French Pro-Consul and dragoman Haji Haroutiun Kassabian, his wife Catherine [Gadar] and his two daughters [Roz and Virjine] were forcibly dragged out of the city and after cruel tortures were put to death. His son, Levon, succeeded in hiding himself in different places in Diyarbekir up to the 7th December 1917, when skilfully disguised as a Kurd he made his escape to the coast and survived to tell the tragic story.

A very large number of Armenian exiles having been killed in the usual brutal manner by the militia and the Kurds at Kozan Dere, a place on the Mardin road, five miles from Diyarbekir, the Committee of Union and Progress had the inspiration to gather all the corpses, dress those of men in Hojah's uniform with turbans on their heads, and those of women with Muslim women's clothing, veils etc. and take several photographs, thousands of copies of which were distributed and sent all over Turkey and Germany to prove most shamefully that the Armenians were to blame for all that had taken place, that Armenian revolutionists and brigands had organised and carried out terrible massacres against the Muslim populations, and that as a result of their conduct the Turkish authorities could hardly control the Kurdish population or assume any responsibility for any outrages possibly committed against the Armenians. While these photographs were being distributed to the Kurds, Arabs and other Muslim races, the most slanderous reports were also put into circulation to excite and provoke all the anger and hatred of those fanatical races against the poor Armenians, who still happened to survive.

Twenty four thousand exiles were tortured and finally killed in
Sheytan Dere (Valley of the Devil) by the Kurdish tribe of Tirkan, who
live a little to the North of Karaja Dagh.* The corpses of the victims
covered a distance of 21 miles between Sheytan Dere and Bogoutlan
[Bigoutlan]. As in other similar cases these corpses were left just in the
same position that they happened to be in when massacred, and for
weeks and months continued to serve as food to birds and beasts.

This dark and infernal period of deportation, exiles and massacres
continued to November 1915.

The few that after all the torture, privations and terrible hardships that
they had been through had strength enough to reach Ras-el-Ain, were left
at the mercy of the uncivilised and wild Circassian natives. They were
treated, as one may expect from such beings, with the utmost
inconsideration, harshness and cruelty, and after many a hard trial they
were taken for imprisonment in the underground dungeons. Many
women and girls willingly threw themselves into these dark, airless
subterranean holes just to escape from the hands of their tormentors. And
there in the midst of utter darkness and among the heaped up and
decaying corpses they had to fight for the preservation of their lives. How
some of them actually escaped and subsequently reached Aleppo is the
greatest of modern miracles. The following three sisters belong to the few
that struggled, wrestled and fought with death, and finally escaped from
its claws, reaching Aleppo in a half-starved, half-dead condition:

Vartouhi (24 years old), Hermine (21 years old), and Takouhie
(19 years old) Kafafian. They survived to show the scars that the tyrant's
rifles, swords and bayonets had left on their bodies and faces. These living
martyrs, deformed and stripped of their former beauty, relate such stories
that no human mind can conceive. History keenly feels the shame that
such unheard of atrocities have to fill many a black page.

Can any body tell what the Kozan and Sheytan Valleys of Diyarbekir,
the Bezwan Valley of Shkefta, the Wawaile [Oudweyle] Valley of

---

* The Armenian text is more precise and says that the killings took place near
the village of Kaynagh —A.S.

Mardin, the deep Roman dungeons of Dara, and the bottomless wells of Ras-el-Ain see? Can any one picture the savage and horrible scenes of atrocities of which they were the silent spectators? How many thousand corpses of men and women and children whom wild beings with human forms refused to spare did they welcome into their cold, damp, lifeless bosom? How many thousand martyrs' bones still cover them?

The Circassians of Ras-el-Ain had the unique idea to cut the hair of the women and girls whom they killed and knit them into 25 meters' long rope of three inches in diameter, which they presented to their worthy Apollyon Feizy Bey. This ghastly reminder of the atrocities committed against Armenians constitutes one of the most appreciated ornaments of this modern hero's house and speaks well of the part which he played in this drama.

Dr. Ismail Bey's Exile

Four hundred orphans, from one to two years old,[*] were deemed worthy in the sight of the executioners to be spared, and so they were gathered and transferred to the Protestant school of Diyarbekir where they were pretty decently looked after for a few months. But suddenly on a certain morning 200 of them were taken to a bridge on the Tigris, built by the Saracens, a little to the South of Diyarbekir, and there they were seized one by one by the head, or arm, or leg and hurled into the fast flowing waters of the Tigris. The remaining 200 were taken a few days later to the village of Karabash, at a five miles' distance from Diyarbekir, and there another most hideous crime was committed. Some of the babies were seized by their legs and pulled in opposite direction so forcibly that they were torn in two. On others the sharpness of the swords or bayonets of their butchers were tried, and real competitions were started as to who could cut at one stroke an arm or a leg or a head or even the baby's body. Others were thrown in the air and caught on lances, while others were thrown to some exceptionally wild shepherd-dogs to be torn to pieces. The official representatives of the Turkish government who assisted at

---

[*] The Armenian text states between one and three —A.S.

Saracens' Bridge, south of Diyarbekir

this heinous scene were most delighted and followed the whole procedure with perfect satisfaction.

There was, however, one man who was overwhelmed with the enormity of the crime: the Inspector of Public Health for the vilayet of Diyarbekir, Dr. Ismail Bey. Unable to contain his feelings of repugnance at what had been going on he said to a circle of friends, "God may forgive all sins, all the massacres, all the atrocities which the Turks committed against the Armenians, but he will never, never, never forgive them for what they did to those innocent, blameless little babies. The day is coming when Turkey, if not for anything else, at least for this one crime, will be wiped out of existence, and she will well deserve the punishment!" A few days after this frank discussion Dr. Ismael Bey, though a Turk, was officially dismissed from his post, and sent together with his family, under escort to Constantinople.

We are told in the Bible that the Tigris, together with the Euphrates watered God's Garden of Eden for Adam. History tells that in days long gone by, when the old uncivilised nations inhabiting its banks were not as cruel as are the Turks of to-day, the Tigris watered happy and prosperous lands and brought riches unto them. In 1915 for days and weeks and months the waters of the Tigris brought down nothing but corpses of the massacred Armenians and watered the land with tears of blood. Its sweet, pure, crystal waters for more than six months flowed mingled with blood, and heaped nothing but corpses at every curve of the river. For six months the city of Diyarbekir beheld the endless string of corpses passing through her very heart and going down, ever down. The Kurds did not drink the water of the river for it was tainted with the blood of the victims that they threw in, nor did they taste the delicious fish, for in their stomach they found human hairs and small bones.

A Few of the Defenders of Diyarbekir

It is to be regretted that the Armenians of Diyarbekir, owing to a divided opinion, were not able to present any resistance as they did in 1895 when for three days they bravely held their own and saved the situation. Hundreds of Kurds and Turkish soldiers who attacked then were killed and the Armenians saved themselves and their honour. It gives one pain to realise that in 1915 Diyarbekir meekly knelt down and surrendered to the villains. One feels bitterly disappointed that Amsih Kazazian, the hero of 1895, who for fifteen whole days shut himself up in his own house refusing to accept anybody's orders, who fought and defended and saved the particular quarter where his house was and the thousands of Armenians who had fled thither for refuge [against thousands of soldiers and gendarmes led by Feizy's father, Arif Effendi], should at this most critical moment hesitate to stand on the height of grandeur and majesty where his former conduct had placed him and lose his courage and heart.

Yet there were a few – only a few – who shine in the midst of encircling gloom, by having made a splendid record of bravely and having saved themselves, their families and their followers. Those men had confidence in themselves and in their bravery, and without ever losing courage carried out successfully the most desperate of attempts. Let me mention a few:

Mardinli Mardo, Hazroli Giragos, Zarzavachi Minjo, Ispiroglou Mardo. These carried a rifle and a revolver each, resisted for days and weeks and even years. They were ever changing their positions, hiding from hole to hole, from cavity to cavity, from well to well. During these long months they fought against the Turks, the Kurds and their associates, as well as against hunger, nakedness and cold weather. Though continually persecuted by their pursuers, they never lost hope but using their rifles honestly, they saved as many as had the courage to throw their fate in with theirs.

Mardinli Mardo once found himself in a very strait position. A spy had discovered his whereabouts and reported it to the authorities, receiving for his services a large reward. Approximately 2,000 men from the militia, police, gendarmes, Kurds, etc. under Major Yasin Zade Shefki Bey surrounded his place and sent one of Mardo's old friends, Sersem Ohno, to persuade him and his followers to come out of their hiding place. Ohno assured him that in case of surrender the Governor and the authorities as well as Major Shefki had under oath promised to spare their lives. Mardo, altogether unaffected by the offer, made the following cutting reply: "Ohno, you are as stupid as your name (*sersem*) signifies. Do not believe any promise of these d—d liars. They are born liars. You had better join me or get away from here. You are an Armenian and a poor man and I don't care killing you." Ohno repeated his answer to Major Shefki Bey, who then ordered him to enter a second time Mardo's hiding place and pull him out by force! On re-entering Ohno was shot dead.

Up to the end of 1917 several dozens of Armenian young men managed in a similar manner to keep themselves alive. They passed from house to house, and from roof to roof, and from cellar to cellar. Every hole and every available mouse-nest, garden, orchard, well, cemetery and every corner of the old walls on the banks of the Tigris were fully utilised by them as places of refuge. They had to steal if getting back part of their own seized property can be so termed, and they often had to fight to save their lives, hiding like mice and lizards, nay, defending themselves like lions and heroes that they might not only save their skin, but that they might also raise the traditional national standard of bravery of the Armenian. Such heroes deserve all honour and glory.

A Celebrated Archbishop and the Offer of a Candle to the Holy Virgin by a Venerable Lady

Chaldean Archbishop of Diyarbekir, Mutran Suleiman.

There also existed a number of Armenians young men who for a considerable time remained in hiding in the city and in the vicinity of Diyarbekir, such as those who had never appeared to join the Turkish army, or had run away from labour corps, or had openly resisted the authorities during the last massacres. Those men lived on some kind of help or other which they received at times from such town people as had pity on them, or were afraid of them and so helped them to prevent further troubles. The greatest difficulty of these "desperadoes" was naturally how to obtain their food, because they had neither homes to use as stores nor were they left at ease by the authorities, who forever pressed hard upon them. Large numbers of soldiers, militia men, gendarmes, police, Kurds and Circassians, and legions of spies allowed them no shelter. Capital punishment or imprisonment for life awaited him who dared help or feed any of the Armenian deserters. On the other hand, large rewards were promised to anyone who could point out definitely the whereabouts of such men.

It was during this reign of terror that a venerable Chaldean was seen every morning and evening going to the "Mar Putim" (St. Peter's) Church, where after lighting a candle in front of the Icon of the Virgin Mary, she would kneel and pray. When, before communion she went once to the Father Confessor, for the regular Confession and found herself obliged to tell him everything, she revealed to him her secret and why she went daily to light a candle in the church. She went on and told him how she had let some Armenian deserters into her house, where she hid them in an out-of-the-way hole of her cellar and fed them as regularly as her means allowed her. The Father Confessor was a rather inexperienced man and felt quite troubled about this matter. He immediately reported it to the Bishop Mutran Suleiman. This Archbishop was really a true shepherd for the sheep committed to his care, a man "without guile," brave and undaunted. He at once sent for her and made her repeat her story. He then told her never to leave her house again but to remain there and take good care of those helpless men, adding, "You have done a great noble deed, which is most acceptable in the sight of God and the Holy Virgin. This will become a stepping stone for you when you leave this world, and will lead you straight to the bosom of the Madonna." After these words he pronounced the absolution of her sins and gave her Communion. When he sent her away to continue her noble duty he told her that if she ever was in need of any money for those men, she could find in him a ready assistant.

May such clergymen live forever, for they are the glory of the Church and the true servants of Christ. May such old pious ladies, true worshipers of the Virgin Mary, live for ever.

A Fiendish German Officer

A Kurd of Mardin, from the tribe of Meshkin, carried away as the best part of the spoils allotted to him after the massacres a beautiful girl of the wealthy family of Arousian. This girl was a graduate of the Franciscan Sisters' High School in Diyarbekir and had a perfect knowledge of the French language. Hearing that there was a German Major in charge of the automobile column in Diyarbekir and quite an influential man with the Turkish authorities, she took the courage to address him a letter in French, in which she gave details of her awful condition and implored him for Christ's sake to intercede with the authorities and save her. He immediately replied that he would be very glad to take her away from the Kurd, provided she became his mistress after her return to Diyarbekir. Without even taking the slightest consideration of this offer, Miss Arousian replied disdainfully that she preferred to remain the wife of an uneducated, villainous Kurd than become the mistress of such a godless, fiendish, infidel German officer as he was!

It was this same profligate German Officer who had changed the Armenian church of Sourp Sarkis into a garage for his automobiles. It was this same person who with complete disregard for all pious feelings not only for Christians but also of Muslims trampled under his feet all sacredness and sanctity of the House of God, while the remorseless heart, "Made in Germany" urged him to authorise his men to make latrine accommodation within the church walls!

There was another Armenian church, the big ancient Cathedral of St. Giragos, famous for its seven altars, which was situated in the quarter of Fatih Pasha. This particular quarter was known among the Muslim population as "Giavour Mahallesi" (The Infidels' Quarter) after the brave defence which the Armenians held there in 1896. The Germans did not hesitate to profane this beautiful cathedral and to change it into their headquarters. The German headquarters' staff closed their eyes and ears to everything that was said or done against the Armenians and their property, and when the pretty steeple of this church, which alone had cost the Armenians 2,000 Turkish Pounds, was pulled down, they did not as much as raise their small finger to protest against its destruction by the Muslims.

These are the words of the acrimonious Germans, the hypocrites, from whom the poor Christians of Turkey, hard pressed and persecuted on every side, dared to expect some help and relief.

The Losses of the Armenians in the Vilayet of Diyarbekir

The Armenian population of the vilayet of Diyarbekir totaled close to 150,000 people. An itemised list of the Armenian population of this vilayet with names and numbers of every village in detail is contained in my still unpublished works "Statistics of the Armenians in the Vilayet of Diyarbekir."[*] This book was complied after many and lengthy efforts and special explorations and researches. It gives the names, sites, historical

---

[*] Unfortunately there is no trace of this manuscript to date. —A.S.

records, inscriptions, etc. of all the Armenian old and new monasteries throughout the vilayet. Also numbers and dates of the Imperial Firmans for their foundation, names of Bishops, priests and teachers, and the number of students. It further gives full information about the lands owned and cultivated by Armenians.

In accordance with the information personally collected from the survivors of Diyarbekir who are still in Aleppo, the number of Armenians massacred in the city of Diyarbekir alone amounts to 25-26,000 souls, while those killed in the provinces amount to 60-65,000, making a total of 91,000, which in other words means that 69,000 Armenians still drag their weary steps somewhere fighting against famine and poverty and all sorts of diseases with the sole cherished hope of living to build out of the ruins and shape a new and free Armenia.

I am attaching at the end of my story for additional information a list of names of such martyrs and heroes (clergymen, government officials, merchants, etc.) as are personally know to me. The list was compiled also from survivors in Aleppo. A list of survivors with whom I am personally acquainted is also attached in the end.

Conclusion

(1) The Armenians made no attempt to sever their political connections with Turkey. On account of their short sightedness in this matter they were overtaken in such an unprepared state that it was easy for the Turks to carry out without any opposition or difficulty these massacres and crucifixions. The Armenians never imagined that such a catastrophe would ever fall upon their heads.

(2) The Armenian political committees did nowhere in Turkey show any sign of unrest or preparation or organisation to betray the Turks or attack their backs, as the Turks claim in their attempt to expiate themselves. The most important so-called (by the Turks) "revolutionary movement" took place in Van, and to this we can easily give the name of a "self-defence movement" because it was locally organised, all of a sudden, by the local population to defend themselves against the Turks and Kurds. And even there, had the Russian army been a little longer delayed in

advancing every one of the defenders of Van would have been put to death. The self-defence scheme of Ourfa, and Shabin Kara Hissar, was also an organisation under the exigencies of the moment. It was hastily, defectively and very unfavourably organised at a moment of imminent danger. If the Armenian committees had actually, as the Turks claim, made any preparations for defence or resistance or for an act of treachery against the Turks, the Turkish government would have never dared to undertake such massacres and deportation. The Turks knew that the Armenians were unprepared and so they killed easily the unarmed and defenceless population.

(3) The following are responsible for the scheme of deportations and massacres, which was so systematically executed throughout Turkey:

(a) All the civilian and military authorities and officials who co-operated in every respect.

(b) The clubs and members of the Committee of Union and Progress in Constantinople and its branches in every part of Turkey.

(c) The Muslim population of Turkey who on its own consent and for its own interests and satisfaction participated in the massacres, looting, deportations and carrying away forcibly of the Armenians women and girls.

(d) The German people and government, who tolerated, encouraged and adhered to the policy of massacres and deportations. Without Germany's consent Turkey would have never undertaken such a wholesale crime.

(4) Respect and gratitude is placed on record for the very few Turks and Kurds, both civilians and military who, putting themselves in danger, helped and saved a considerable number of Armenians.

(5) We hope and expect that the Peace Conference will take into consideration the number of Armenians before 1914, when the Great War was declared, as well as the number which the Armenians will have as soon as the free and prosperous Armenia of the future will be established, and that they will decide on Armenia's fate accordingly. Any decision to the contrary will again encourage future oppressions and the extermination of weak and defenceless nations.

(6) It is whole-heartedly expected that the survivors of those massacres, as well as the Armenians now scattered all over the world, will consider it their duty and happy obligation to go back to their own homes, whereby putting into use the experience acquired during these dark and bitter days, and with the lesson of mutual co-operation adopted by the Great Allies during this war, they will lay the firm and sound foundations for a political, social, financial and educational life of the re-established free Armenia; that they will organise every branch of the new state in the best possible manner and that by applying the sacred principles of truth, justice, brotherhood and equality to all the races that will be included within the Armenian boundaries, even their murderers of yesterday, they will do honour both to themselves and to the Great Powers who entrusted them with this duty, that they will attract the love and respect of friend and foe alike and will justify the expectations of those who lived, worked, suffered and died, that an altogether free and independent Armenia might forever continue her noble course in the path of prosperity under the cover of God's almighty wing, and with the never failing assistance of the protecting powers.

[PART III]

List of the Most Important Martyrs in the City of Diyarbekir

a. The Consular Party

Dr. Vosgian, Honorary Dragoman of H.B.M.'s Vice Consulate with all family – wife [Shamiram], a girl [Virginia] and a boy [Hovhannes, four]. Only Eftimia, a girl 11 years old, survived. She was recently bought from Memdouh Bey by Sahag Tashjian, an Armenian, who paid 45 pounds for her.*†

b. Religious and Intellectual People

Bishop Mugerdich Chlghadian and nine priests.

Bishop Vahan, the chief of Arakelots Monastery.

Archbishop Andreas Chelebian, Armenian Catholic, and three priests.

Rev. Hagop Andonian, Protestant pastor, [and wife, Mariam].

Forty eight teachers, male and female, of the Armenian Apostolic, Armenian Catholic, and Armenian Protestant schools.

c. The Government Officials

Stepan Chirajian, Parliamentary Deputy.

Jurjis Kazazian. Member of the Provincial Council [and landowner].

Kachadour Dikranian. Member of the Provincial Council.

Dikran Ilvanian. The Dragoman of the Vilayet [and teacher at Idadiye school].

Samuel Hilmi (Assyrian). [First] Secretary of the Vilayet.

Garabed Chirajian, Mudir of Habab [Nahiye].

[Khosrov Chirajian, Secretary to Attorney General]

Haroutiun Minassian, Director of Post Office.

---

* The Armenian text states that Memdouh Bey had bought the girl from Major Shevki for 25 piasters. —A.S.

† The Armenian text also includes in this section Haji Haroutiun Kassabian, French Embassy dragoman and vice-consul, his wife Gadar, and two girls Eozhen and Virjin. —A.S.

Philibbos Arpiarian, Director of Agriculture Bank [native of Kharpert].

Melkon Soukiasian, Director of Agriculture Department.

Hovsep Hakimian, Secretary of Imperial Ottoman Bank.

Boghos Tomoyan, Member of the Municipal Council [and landowner].

Misak Shirigjian, Member of the Municipal Council [and landowner].

Haroutiun Mouradian, Member of the Municipal Council [and landowner].

Garabed Alyanak (Assyrian), Member of the Municipal Council (banker).

Yousouf Papazian (Chaldean), Member of the Municipal Council [and landowner].

Ruskalla Chelebian, Member of the Court of Appeal.

Garabed Khandenian, Member of the [Criminal Court] "Jeza Muhakemesi".

Dikran Jirahian, "Mudai Umumi" [Attorney General].

Garabed Natuk, lawyer and representative of the Ottoman Museum.

Giragos Yenovkian, lawyer [and landowner].

Boghos Der Kaprielian, lawyer [and landowner].

Kevork Keor Oghlian, lawyer [of Lije].

Colonel Dr. Artin Bey Helvajian, [chief surgeon] "Ser Tabib".

Captain Dr. Hovannes Terzian.

Captain Dr. Nishan Bakalian.

Captain Dr. Avedis Bal Manougian (dentist) [native of Aintab].

Hagop Hekimian, pharmacist.

Artin Aghegian, pharmacist.

d. Landowners, Bankers, Merchant, and Other Important People

Kazazian brothers and sons with their whole family.*

Mugerdich, Giragos and Mardig Turpenjian brothers and sons with their families.**

Mugerdich and Haroutiun Yegenian. The whole family. [Landowner].

Garabed and Haji Hagop Khandenian [landowner, shareholder in Pirejman copper mines].

Hovhannes and Dikran Mendeljian [landowners and merchants].

Garabed and Minas Boyajian.

Hagop Karanfilian [landowner].

Haroutiun Mouradian [landowner].

Shiukri and Misak Shirigjian [landowner].

Alexam Jenezian [landowner].

*These bankers lost about 300,000 pounds in value.

**These bankers lost about 280,000 pounds in value.*

e. Silk Manufacturers
Abdalian brothers.

Mugerdich Terekejian.

Mardiros Attarian.

Haroutiun Boyajian.

[Hagop Bakalian.]

Hagop Kazanjian.

f. Merchants
Dikranian Brothers.

Karashian Brothers.

Topalian Brothers.

Stepan Mattosian.

Ajemian Brothers.

Hovannes, Hagop and Dikran Donjian.

Boghos Kazazian.

Bastajian Brothers.

Kaiserlian Brothers.

Bazigian Brothers.

Krekorian Brothers.

Katibian Brothers.

Kalemkerian Brothers.

Mikhael Roumi (Syarian Catholic).

Moumjian Brothers (Syrians).

* The Armenian text says 250,000 and 300,000 respectively. —A.S.

Fathoulla Hakim (Chaldean).
Boudougian Krikor & Sons.
Shukhloian Brothers.
Der Boghossian Brothers [landowners].
Hovsep Shirigjian.
Parseghian Brothers.
Dikran Andonian.
Samuel Bundukian.
Hovannes Voskerijian.
Hagopian Brothers.
Najarian Brothers.
Kasbarian Brothers.
Amsih Sabagh & Sons.
Bedros Hakim (Chaldean banker).
Yorghi Abaji (Greek).
Yussuf Kosti (Greek).
Serraf Vasil (Greek banker).
etc., etc., etc.

List of the Most Important Martyrs in Mardin

Archbishop Ignatios Maloian and all the Maloian family (Armenian Catholic).

Bishop Hovhannes Vartabed Bodourian, Armenian Catholic.

Mugerdich Kahana Kalyonjian, Armenian Catholic.

Seventeen more Armenian priests.

Uskof Selim Jirjis Hass, Protestant pastor.

Killed		Survived
Iskender Adem & family	11	2 girls, Marin & Josephine and a 5 year old grandson
Nahoum Jenanji family	6	2 girls, Shefka and Virgin
Hanna Jenanji	1	wife, Muksie
Amsih Jenanji	1	—
Elias Bahbosa family	12	Elias
Hanna Kendir family		Jubir Kendir and wife
Sahdo Kendir family		—
Fathalla Kendir family		Fatoh, 6 year old son
Raphael Cherme family	10	3 girls, Bahie, Nazlie, Jemil
Sarkis Saidi family		—
Beit Shallume family	25	Katrina, Yacoub
Beit Hailo family	3	3 women and 5 children
Beit Kaspo family	6	Josephine and 2 boys
Boghos Makboulle family	40	Emine and Said
Yussuf Karagoullah family	5	Jemail and Katerina
Said Karagoullah family	1	wife (refugee in Cairo)
Joseph Khuzri	1	wife Marie
Brahim Shankhar	1	father, mother, wife & children
Rev. Jirjis and two brothers	3	father, mother and children
Aziz Kacho	2	—
Hanna Azruk	1	—
Selim Ubrani	4	Ferid, Aziz and three daughters

Ousse Nahme	2	—
Beit Marina	2	—
Avedis Saati	1	wife in Baghdad, daughter in Aleppo
Said Usho	1	—
Rushkalla Hatoune	1	—
Beit Haja Younan	1	family in Aleppo
Beit Churbaka family	16	Ladoys, refugee in Cairo
Mansour Kalyounji	60	Habbo and 2 boys in Cairo
Hanna Murkezeh family	1	—
Beit Manadir family	7	—
Beit Yogho family	4	—
Beit Dokmak family	4	wife alive
Beit Adem family	2	wife alive
Beit Hammal family	3	wife alive
Beit Dilenji family	1	wife alive
Beit Afrit family	2	wife alive
Beit Jirjis Sousi family	10	—
Beit Mertibit family	4	—
Beit Nasri Katurji family	20	—
Beit Shoha family	7	—
Beit Tufenkji family	all	—
Beit Muldosi Kuheb family		women alive
Beit Apre Saigh family	all	—
Beit Mahmar Bashi family	3	women refugee in Aleppo
Beit Ousse Bahe family	1	—
Daoud Kecho	all	—
Said Stamboulli	1	wife and children still in Mardin
Beit Kondagji	2	—

There were about 2,100 families in the city of Mardin alone (Armenian-Catholic and Protestant). Hardly 100 families have survived and of these, each family has sustained some losses.

[PART IV]

Appendix

Supplementary information about the Armenian tribes which were forced to become Kurdish, and the tribes which remained Armenian in spites of all ill-treatment:.

In order to gratify the demand of the present moment, I am submitting in this supplement a short history of all Armenian tribes of the Diyarbekir Province,* which after having been, since 1517, under the yoke of the Tatar-Turk rulers, with the result that they had to change their religion and faith, and did so in order not to abandon their fatherland and be able to safeguard the continuation of their race.

I leave to a more suitable time the publication of a historical study, regarding the above and all Kurdish tribes in Turkey and Yezidis (Devil Worshippers) [sic].

To start with, I will relate about the tribes which I have already mentioned in the historical part of my book, and then will treat the others.

1. RUSHDOUNIK. This is the so-called "Resh Kota" Kurdish sedentary tribe, which dwells in the North of the Busheri District, situated between Batman Sou (Kaghert River) and Revdan Sou (Arzon River). The Reshkota is divided into the following seven sub-tribes — Khasarka, Darmanka, Shekhuka, Baboujanka, Bundurka, Chaluka, and Piroka. I mentioned as under a few of the villages inhabited by the sub-tribes, Salib, Dara-Bi, Dara-Baru, Zedia, Hajina, Lijak, Reshuk, Merina, Khelukan, Durbessan, Bolehd, etc. The country is upland and its soil fertile. The inhabitants occupy themselves mostly with agriculture and sheep breeding. They have their own leaders and every tribesman is a skilled rider and a good shot.

---

* This province was formerly called "Diyarbekir Allayet Eyalet" which also included the provinces of Kharpert and Bitlis. These last two provinces were severed from the province of Diyarbekir in 1878 when Kars and Ardahan passed to Russia following the Treaty of San Stefano.

They never supply any soldiers to the Turkish government, and have preserved up to now their savage and quarrelsome nature. They are only nominally under the control of the Turkish authorities.

2. THE MAMIGONIANS, are called now "Mamiga" tribe and dwell east of the Redvan Sou. They state that they had previously as capital, Arzen, a walled ancient town now in ruins, situated on the eastern bank of Redvan Sou (Arzen Sou) on the main road from Diyarbekir to Bitlis. The soil is naturally irrigated and very fertile. The inhabitants are farmers and shepherds.

One can see up till now, on the Redvan Sou, the remains of a bridge which is most unique from a historical point of view. This is built in a very peculiar way. It has two tunnel roads at both ends and could be traversed, whilst its top was used as a caravan road. This bridge is up to the present time known as Mamiga-bridge and is situated near Silakher village.

A part of the Mamigonian tribe being in the neighbourhood of the biggest and strongest Armenian tribe Khalta, was amalgamated with it, whilst the other part was obliged to relinquish its faith and at present forms the Kurdish tribe Mamiga.

The villages Hop, Doussadek, etc. of Mamigonian origin, succeeded in remaining Armenian through the assistance of the Khalta, the neighbours, but they have lost their language which was Armenian.

3. ALYANS AND THE ALANS, are called at present Alica tribe and are found between the following frontiers, North-West Reshkota, West Bushery, North and North-East Mamiga, and South-East Khalta.

There is another Kurdish tribe called Alyan which is very populous and lives in the Jezire district, south of Jebel-Tor (Masios Mountain). This tribe occupies forty villages.

4. THE MAGWUIS OR MOGWUIS TERRITORY, bears at present the name of Motga Kurdish tribe. The land inhabited by the tribe is a continuation of Adok (mount Taurus). Its upland is woody and fertile. The boundaries are: North, the main road from Moush to Bitlis; East, the main road from Bitlis to Zor; South, Gherzan tribe; and West, Sassoon.

This tribe is very strong and every tribesman is a good rider and shot. It is the same tribe which assaulted Bitlis in March 1914, occupied the town after having driven out the Turkish authorities and succeeded in ruling the town for about a fortnight when they yielded to a strong force sent from Van.*

The Turkish government sentenced to death thirteen of the leaders and partisans of this movement and thus the drama came to an end.

5. THE ARMENIANS OF MASIOS MOUNTAINS. These mountains, inhabited formerly by Armenians and Syrians, bear now the name of Tor-Abdin (Mountain of Monks).

The Armenians and Jacobites relinquished their faith under the leadership of the Syrian patriarch Ismayel and formed the Kurdish tribe Muhallemi.

The archives of Deir-Zaaferan monastery relate that "Patriarch Ismayel was summoned to Constantinople by the Turkish Sultan and made 'Sheikh Ismayel'. He was there much favoured and returned to his country with many presents. He became the leader of his tribe which he organised and exterminated later on all his enemies."

6. ASHDIK AND HASHDIANK. On the South and Western banks of the Tigris is a very powerful and crowded Kurdish tribe, Ashiti, which dwells North and East of Tor-Abdin (Mount Masios). Certain churches and singular signs such as crosses are engraved on the walls, buildings and caves of the villages of Hassankeff, situated on the bank of the Tigris, and in some other Kurdish villages, which bear ample evidence that the people who lived there were Christians and there is every reason to believe that they were Armenians of the Ashdi and Hashdiank tribes.

The Kurds of the Ashiti tribes themselves confess that their ancestors were "giavours" (infidels) and were later on converted to the "Hak Din" (Mohammedan True Faith).

---

* This may be a popular notion of what happened in Bitlis 1914. However, this rebellion was crushed when the attacking Kurdish tribes failed to gain control of the city and its arsenal. —A.S.

The Ashiti Kurds are divided into two sub-tribes – Hawerki and Bakshuri. The tribesman are farmers, shepherds and vine cultivators. They are good fighters but brigands and are only nominally under the Turkish rule.

7. YEGUEGHIATS (Churches). There is a noted Kurdish tribe called Dour-Dor, which is continually wandering in the provinces of Diyarbekir, Mosul and Bitlis. Dour-Dor means two churches. This proves that the people were Christians belonging to the Yegueghiats tribe.

The Dour-Dor tribesmen are cattle breeders and possess a considerable number of mules. They have been masters of commercial transport between the three above mentioned provinces and Aleppo.

The Dour-Dor tribesman being docile and energetic [sic] are called "Kurdish giavours" (infidels) by the other Kurds.

8. HOUN. This is a sedentary tribe dwelling in Pala-Hovid (Cherry Valley) situated South East of Palu. There is also a village bearing the name of Houn, which is on the southern bank of Mourad Sou at four hours' distance from Palu. Houn is the capital of a tribe of the same name. The meaning of the word in the Armenian language is the "Passage of River".

There are many other villages still bearing Armenian names with a slight confusion with the Kurdish language, viz, "Akrag", "Akarag", "Sera-Chour", "Sari-Chour", "Budghik", "Budghik" [sic], etc.

The leaders of this tribe confess that their ancestors were "giavours" [infidels] and embraced the "Hak Din".

9. SORA. There is in the district of Sert, Bitlis province, a tribe called Sora living up till now with another Kurdish tribe bearing the same name.

10. GESS AND GUESSAN (Half and Halves). This is one name of a Kurdish sedentary tribe dwelling in the Diyarbekir province in the district of Chermoug with Guesse-Guiz (Sorrowful) as its main village. The inhabitants of this village are half Armenian and half Kurdish. A curious and interesting feature is that most of the families have half of their members as Mohammedans and the other half as Armenian-

Christians. The Armenian priest regularly visits every family of the village, baptises and confirms every child without distinction of creed. He also pays a visit to the families every new year and on every feast, when he blesses the house, the salt and the bread. Furthermore, he initiates everybody in the family and gives them the Holy Communion.

The Molla, the Muslim priest, also visits the families, circumcises only the Mohammedan males, and give some lectures on the Mohammedan faith. The term Guesse-Guiz, (that is Sorrowful) is very appropriately assigned to this tribe.

The greater part of this tribe became Kurdish and is residing now in the South of Severek district, together with the Kurdish nomadic tribe Kara-Kechi, and bears the name of Guessan (in Armenian, the Halves).

The male members of this tribe and those of the Kara-Kechi form the 44th regiment of the "Hamidie" cavalry.

11. TAYAN. There is an Armenian nomadic tribe living with a Kurdish tribe of the same name. For this reason it is generally believed that both are of Kurdish origins. They both dwell in the Suloupi district, situated in the Kardoukhi (Gortouadz) Mountains, North East of the Tigris.

The Tayan tribe journeys every summer to Van province and returns in the autumn with their cattle and herds, wandering continually between the Sinjar Mountains and the Tigris.

Up to the beginning of the Great War, Der Tateos, an Armenian priest from Jezireh used to visit this tribe twice a year; once in the spring, when people crossed the Tigris on their way to Van province, the second time in the Autumn, when the tribe was on its return journey to its winter home.

During this biennial visits, this priest used to Christen children, perform wedding services, pray for the dead, bless the leaven bread, the salt and the herds, administer Holy Communion, and comfort every body by giving two pieces of host to each.

May I commit the indiscretion of saying that a pious Hagop Agha Kouyoumjian, a native of Gesaria [Kayseri], who was residing in Diyarbekir and left for Baghdad after the Armenian massacres of 1895, had allotted a certain amount to be paid annually to this anchorite, Der Tateos, who continued his mission conscientiously.

12. DERSIM. This district is in the anti-Taurus Mountains and lies between the rivers Euphrates, Mourad-Sou and Keghi-Sou. Dersim district included the kazas of Ovajik, Kouzijan, Mazgerd (Medzgerd in Armenian), Kizil-Kilise (Red Monastery), Pakh and Kozat, the latter is the main town of the district. Dersim nominally began to yield to Turkish rule in 1848 (Hegira 1264). The first kaimakam was known to the natives by the name of Miussellim and had the main village of Ovajik Kaza as his centre.[*] Kozat became the centre of all Dersim in 1881, when the district was changed into a vilayet. The first Vali was a native Kurdish leader named Fikri Pasha. He and his two successors ruled two years each, when the Turkish government got disgusted with the unruly Dersim Kurds. The province was changed into Mutasseriflik in 1887[†] (Hegira 1303) and annexed to the Mamouret-ul-Aziz vilayet. However, Dersim never obeyed the vexatious Turkish yoke. It always remained hostile.

There is evidence that Dersim was in ancient times the heart of Greater Armenia from the religious point of view. Perhaps no other Armenian district ever had so numerous monasteries and convents. It is sufficient to mention only ten monasteries of the twenty six which were built in ancient times in Dersim province.

(1) Sourp Medzn Nerses Pontiff's Monastery, which contains the tomb of St. Nerses the Great, situated near Ki, a Greek village. St. Nerses the Great was the grandson of St. Krikor Lousavorich (St. Gregory the Illuminator).

(2) Sourp Giragos Monastery, built on the heights surrounding Kour village.

(3) Sourp Kevork Monastery built in Yergna village.

(4) Charcharanats Lousavorich Monastery, built in the Mirjan Pass. In this monastery is the dungeon in which the Pontiff St. Krikor the Illuminator was maltreated.

---

[*] The Armenian text names this centre as Zereng village. —A.S.

[†] The Armenian text has this date as 1886. —A.S.

(5) Sourp Nigoghos Monastery in Putaraj village.

(6) Sourp Boghos Monastery in Chakhurmoun village.

(7) Sourp Garmir Monastery in Garmir village.

(8) Sourp Shogha Monastery in Shogha village.

(9) Medz Lousavorich Monastery built at the foot of Sebouh Mountain.

(10) Sourp Louys monastery built on the top of Sub Lous Mountain.* etc.

All this evidence proves that there were once numerous Armenians residing in the Dersim district. Many people believe that the Dersim Kurdish tribes are Armenians of the Terchan tribe. I leave this to be proved by more capable authorities. I should like to mention that the author of this booklet has been able to see, embrace and kiss the crown and silk flag of an Armenian royalty, which were in the possession of the most famous leaders of Dersim Kurdish tribes. These relics were kept as most precious treasures inherited from the ancestors.

13. KHALTA. This is the strongest and most numerous tribe which has succeeded up to the present in maintaining its subsistence, national customs, rights and traditions. The tribesmen have always been guided by "Melik" Kaloyan (Kalousdian) family in a prudent and democratic way.†

Although the Khalta tribe was from 1830 to 1850 victims to religious fanaticism and to the bandits of Sheikh Jelal-el-Din [Jellaleddin], and was on two further occasions attacked by the tyrannical and ferocious Bohdan Kurds under the leadership of the Bedirkhans who raided the Khaltas with the object of converting them to Islam, the Khaltas succeeded in repulsing the first two attacks with great losses; but the third raid, which was under the leadership of Azdin-Sher, the uncle of Bedirkhan Pasha, ‡ was avoided by the tactful policy of Melik Mahdesi Kalo Kaloyan, who

---

* "Sourp Louys Mountain" is called "Sub-Lous" by Kurds.

† The Armenian text names this family as "Melik Mahdesi Kaloyentsi (Kalousdian)." —A.S.

‡ The Armenian text says "the paternal uncle of Abdulkhan Beg." —A.S.

got rid of the marauders by giving them presents and a large sum of money, thus sparing his tribe the horrors of invasion.

The writer remembers that in 1877 Azdin-Sher and Bahri Bey (the latter being the son of Bedirkhan) amassed over 10,000 Bohdan Kurds, went past Khalta with the authorisation of the tribe of the same name, and raided the Alikan Kurds whom they exterminated.

The Khalta had the following three other sub-tribes which live in complete harmony with each other and with the main tribe.

(1) **Mamigan,** which is half-Armenian and half-Kurd.

(2) **Penjinar.** The majority are Kurds and the remainder Armenian. This sub-tribe is in close communication with the Khaltas of whom it is an off-spring.

(3) **Bamerd.** This sub-tribe is also half-Kurd and half-Armenian, and dwells in the lands near the mouth of Redvan Sou, which flows into the Tigris and from there to Bohdan Sou (Gindridis river).

The centre of the Khalta tribe is Redvan, situated on the bank of Redvan Sou. It possesses a high fortress of lime and stone, but all are in ruins now. The Khaltas began paying taxes to the Turkish government in 1870. In the beginning each male over 20 years of age used to pay a annual tax called Kharaj. The following are some of the villages: Khanuk, Silekher Dousha, Mrdesi, Bumbaruk, Upper and Lower Soulan, Miluka, Khundouk, Jumsarib, Arenz, Zakhoran, Benarin, etc. Each village has its headman forming, so to speak, a kind of senate under the Melik, the leader of the tribe. This council decides upon all cases of the tribe.

There are up till now in Jezireh, Sanjar, Ourfa, and Marash, some branches of the Khalta tribe which were deported long ago owing to various disturbances and other events, subjugated and forced to embrace the Muslim faith.

The Khalta tribe, although of Armenian origin, lost its mother tongue and now speaks Kurdish. However, it is noteworthy that the American Missionaries and the Armenian Miatsyal Society have opened a school in Redvan and Hop villages so that everyone under 30 years of age knows Armenian.

14. There are many other tribes partly Armenian and partly Kurdish:

(a) **Silivan** district, Mufarghin[*] being the centre, there are two big tribes called Sulev and Zuruka. These two sedentary tribes possess besides the Kurdish villages sixty four large towns peopled by Armenians who are proprietors of the lands.

(b) **Busheri** district is peopled by Sunuka and Rejeban tribes occupying besides the Kurdish villages twenty five towns whose inhabitants are all Armenians and landowners. The Armenian Miatsyal and the Armenian General Benevolent Union have opened schools in these districts so that the new generation speaks the Armenian tongue. It should be also mentioned that almost all the Kurdish tribes in general contain a considerable number of Armenian members.

There is need to explain that in all Kurdish speaking tribes, the Church service is held in the old classical Armenian language.

I will conclude by stating that all the aforesaid tribes possess up till now traditions, customs and habits proving amply and evidently that they were of Armenian origin and that they lost their faith and religion by force or by other oppressive means.

In support of my statement I will relate some interesting features with regards to traditions of the said tribes.

(1) The Dersim, Baduka, Bekira, Reshkota, Mamuga, Aluka, etc. tribes contain names such as "Mala-Mutran" Bishop's family; "Mala-Keshe" the priest's family; "Mala-Mucho" the Mugerdich family; "Mala-Kalo" the Kalousd family; "Mala-Suho" the Sahag family; "Mala-Muko" the Melkon family; "Mala-Mikho" the Mikaael family; "Mala-Suko" the Serkis family; "Mala-Ono" the Hovhannes family; "Mala-Tukho" the

---

* Mufarghin (in Armenian called Nëpergerd and Mardirosats Kaghak) is an ancient walled Armenian town which, according to tradition, was built by Dikranouhi, sister of the Armenian king, Dikran the Great. The legend says that Dikranouhi boasted presumptuously to her brother that the town Nëpergerd, which she had built, was so strong that it could not be destroyed either by man or God. King Dikran, who feared God, replied that his Dikranagerd (Diyarbekir) was so strong that nobody could destroy it except God. This is why the Diyarbekir walls exist now whilst the walls of Mufarghin are in ruins.

Toukhman family; "Mala- Sumo" the Simon family; "Mala-Fullah" the Christian family, etc.

(2) The women when preparing their bread make on the dough two curves in the shape of a cross which is filled after fermentation, showing that the leaven is ready. This is an old custom of Armenians only. Most of the men and women in the above mentioned Kurdish tribe cross themselves when seeing the sunrise or lightning and say "Sos-Krisdos" (Hisous Krisdos – Jesus Christ).

(3) At full moon and sometimes in the first quarter of the moon, babies fall ill and have sore lashes. The Kurdish mother traditionally makes a cross with black on the forehead, the breast, and the back of the child, convinced that this will avoid the evil eye and the influence of the devil.

(4) On New Year's eve (which is called "Lole" by Armenians and Kurds) it is customary for the people to go to the river or spring and have a cold bath, believing that (a) the merciful God would diffuse on them gold instead of water; and that all those who are present at that moment might possess a great fortune; (b) that all those who bathe at that moment remain clean all year round and exempt from diseases. This is also traditional amongst Armenians.

(5) At Easter Kurds dye eggs with red colours and play with them. This is an exclusively Christian custom which Kurds imitate.

(6) Not only the tribes mentioned in this appendix, but also the Teruka and Nerib, who are Zaza Kurds, call up till now the watered corn "Chërpos," the drain "Aghpin," and the vine-press "Hedzan". All these words are purely Armenian.

(7) The above mentioned tribes in particular and all tribes in general profess a great respect for the Armenian sacred places and especially the monastery of Sourp Garabed at Moush, which they call Dera-Chengelli (the Belled Monastery) and Khana-Poutuke (the Monastery of Good Luck). The Kurds visit these places in the same spirit as the Armenians and offer gifts with the same convictions.

The rope-dancers visit once a year the villages of both Armenians and Kurds. The latter call these travelling rope dancers "Palawane Khana Poutuke" (the "Dancers of Good Luck.") These dancers wear under their arms a certain talisman of Sourp Garabed. Like the Armenians, the Kurds are surprised at Saint Garabed's miraculous power which protects these rope dancers when dancing on rope.

The Kurds, whether male or female, sing songs in the praise of the miraculous influence of Sourp Garabed and his power.

Kurdish girls, like Armenian beauties, are animated by the same conviction and ask for the luck brought by Sourp Garabed in granting them gallant sweethearts.

The Kurds go so far as to swear by Saint Garabed and offer gifts to collectors from the monasteries, especially those of Sourp Garabed, who are never refused.

Is it necessary to wonder and visit museums and other places of this description in order to collect evidence; is history not repeating itself [sic]?

The horrible events of 1895 which took place in Anatolia in the six Armenian vilayets are and should still be fresh and alive in the memory of everybody, when in the vilayet of Aleppo, in many villages and districts, and particularly in the district of Belejik, every individual Armenian embraced the Mohammedan religion under the terror of the massacres of his co-religionists and the tyranny and oppression of the Turks. These Armenians of whom the males were already circumcised, returned to their previous faith under the protection of and with the assistance of Mr. FitzMaurice, the Political Advisor of the British Embassy, who went to the spot in 1896 provided with the necessary Firmans from the Sultan.

Also in the vilayet of Diyarbekir about 30,000 Armenians had embraced the Mohammedan religion under the same nefarious influence but they succeeded in returning to their previous faith, thanks to the protection of the British Consulate of Diyarbekir, which formed a mission empowered by Firmans from Constantinople under the presidency of the writer.

It is necessary to mention any of the events which occurred during the terrible plague, which shook the whole world in 1914 to 1918, in that hell which bears the name of Turkey, where over one million Armenians were slaughtered by the ferocious Turks, where heart-breaking incidents continue up till now in spite of the hopes of peace which were never realised. Part of the survivors were obliged to embrace the Mohammedan religion and all are now living under the terror and tyranny of the slaughterers. Was it not the fear of the Allies, who have at heart the protection of small and weak nations, the ferocious Turks would have carried out their plans which were to exterminate the whole Armenian nation.

(8) Besides the Dersim relics, the writer had on a second opportunity to see and kiss the crown and silk flag of the Pakradouni royalty, which were in the possession of a famous Kurdish leader of one of the above mentioned tribes. A proposal of several hundred pounds was made some years ago by the writer to the holder for the purchase of these relics but the half-savage but intelligent and far sighted leader refused the offer making the following prophecy, "The day shall come when despotism will be destroyed, tyranny and oppression disappear, and religion be free. Then through these sacred relics I shall be able to prove that I am a descendant of Armenian royalty, when I shall have the right to be reinstated in the inheritance of my forefathers.

In this connection it is useful to mention that we Armenians have a delicate and responsible duty to act in future, individually, in a circumspect way and with foresight. We should be an example to all the surrounding communities and races of whom many are waiting anxiously for an opportunity to throw themselves in the arms of the Mother Church and Mother Land.

END

Gomidas Institute - Western Armenian Transliteration System

Ա ա	a		Շ շ	sh	
Բ բ	p		Ո ո	o, vo	
Գ գ	k		Չ չ	ch, ch'	
Դ դ	t		Պ պ	b	
Ե ե	e, ye		Ջ ջ	ch	
Զ զ	z		Ռ ռ	r, rr	
Է է	e		Ս ս	s	
Ը ը	u, ë		Վ վ	v	
Թ թ	t, t'		Տ տ	d	
Ժ ժ	j		Ր ր	r	
Ի ի	i		Ց ց	ts, ts'	
Լ լ	l		Ւ ւ	v	
Խ խ	kh		Փ փ	p, p'	
Ծ ծ	dz		Ք ք	k, k'	
Կ կ	g		և	yev, ev	
Հ հ	h		Օ օ	o	
Ձ ձ	ts		Ֆ ֆ	f	
Ղ ղ	gh				
Ճ ճ	j				
Մ մ	m				
Յ յ	h				
Ն ն	n				

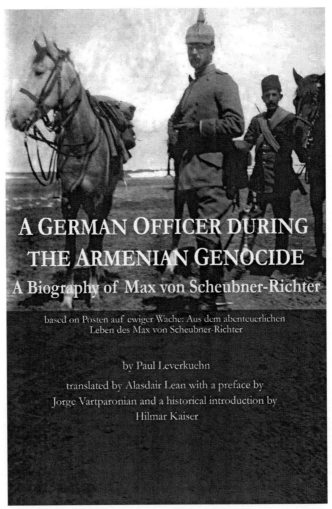

A GERMAN OFFICER DURING THE ARMENIAN GENOCIDE
A Biography of Max von Scheubner-Richter

based on Posten auf ewiger Wache: Aus dem abenteuerlichen
Leben des Max von Scheubner-Richter

by Paul Leverkuehn

translated by Alasdair Lean with a preface by
Jorge Vartparonian and a historical introduction by
Hilmar Kaiser

Paul Leverkuehn, *A German Officer During the Armenian Genocide: A Biography of Max von Scheubner-Richter,* London: Gomidas Institute, 2009.

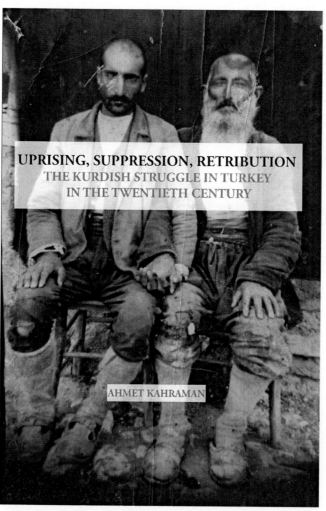

UPRISING, SUPPRESSION, RETRIBUTION
THE KURDISH STRUGGLE IN TURKEY
IN THE TWENTIETH CENTURY

AHMET KAHRAMAN

Ahmet Kahraman, *Uprising, Suppression, Retribution: the Kurdish Struggle in Turkey in the Twentieth Century,* London: Parvana, 2007.

GOMIDAS INSTITUTE
www.gomidas.org

Lightning Source UK Ltd.
Milton Keynes UK
UKOW03f2010300114

225611UK00001B/12/P